AMERICAN RAILROAD JOURNAL

1966

AMERICAN RAILROAD JOURNAL

Golden West Books

San Marino, California

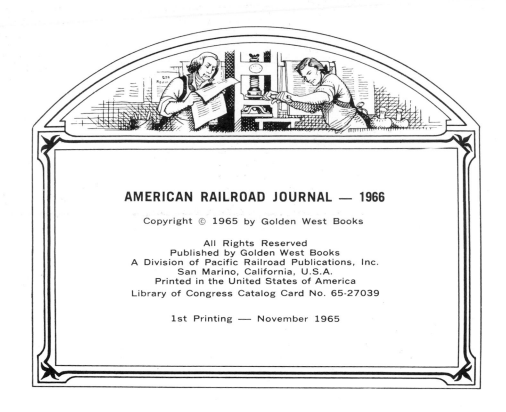

THE COVER ILLUSTRATION — Most of Nevada's romantic short line railroads were built to serve remote and inaccessible mining treasures. Ever since the days of the fabled bonanza mines, the Nevada Northern Railway has served the large scale open pit mining operations of southern Nevada. This 164-mile common carrier line connects with the Western Pacific at Cobre and the Southern Pacific at Shafter. Owned by the Kennecott Copper Company, the Nevada Northern handles several trains of bullion per week, while the mining railroad operates more than 10 trains per day between the copper pit and smelter. The primitive nature of the Nevada Northern countryside may be seen on the cover illustration. Green boilered No. 40, a Baldwin ten-wheeler rolls into Cherry Creek station for water on a warm afternoon. — DONALD DUKE PHOTOGRAPH

Golden West Books

A Division of Pacific Railroad Publications, Inc.

P.O. BOX 8136 • SAN MARINO, CALIFORNIA • 91108

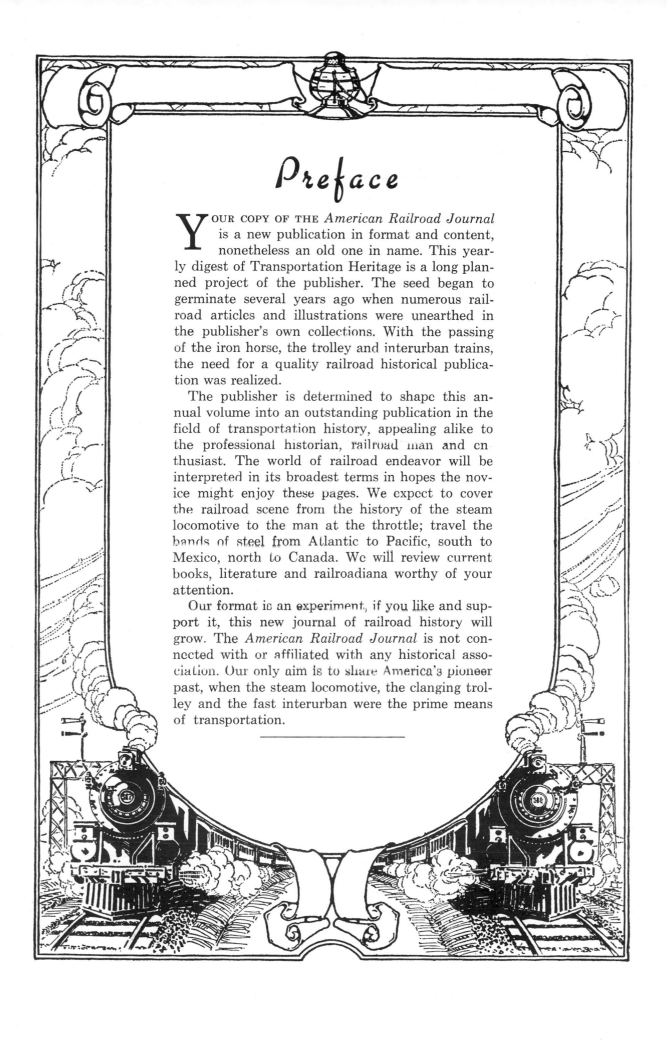

Preface

Your copy of the *American Railroad Journal* is a new publication in format and content, nonetheless an old one in name. This yearly digest of Transportation Heritage is a long planned project of the publisher. The seed began to germinate several years ago when numerous railroad articles and illustrations were unearthed in the publisher's own collections. With the passing of the iron horse, the trolley and interurban trains, the need for a quality railroad historical publication was realized.

The publisher is determined to shape this annual volume into an outstanding publication in the field of transportation history, appealing alike to the professional historian, railroad man and enthusiast. The world of railroad endeavor will be interpreted in its broadest terms in hopes the novice might enjoy these pages. We expect to cover the railroad scene from the history of the steam locomotive to the man at the throttle; travel the bands of steel from Atlantic to Pacific, south to Mexico, north to Canada. We will review current books, literature and railroadiana worthy of your attention.

Our format is an experiment, if you like and support it, this new journal of railroad history will grow. The *American Railroad Journal* is not connected with or affiliated with any historical association. Our only aim is to share America's pioneer past, when the steam locomotive, the clanging trolley and the fast interurban were the prime means of transportation.

The masthead of the new weekly publication changed periodically and often illustrated the principal editorial feature. The issue on the left described the new English steam carriage.—SMITHSONIAN INSTITUTION

AMERICAN
Railroad Journal - 1832

RAILROAD TRAVEL in the United States was in its infancy when the first issue of the *American Railroad Journal* left the New York pressroom January 1, 1832. Steam locomotives were hardly more than a boiler mounted on a flat rail car, and passengers rode in carriages with railroad wheels affixed.

The first issue contained the following article, "The subscriber proposes to publish a weekly Journal, commencing about the first of January, ensuing, to be called the *American Railroad Journal*. A principal object in offering the proposed work to the Public, is to diffuse a more general knowledge of this important mode of internal communication, which, at this time, appears to engage the attention of almost every section of our country.

"The *American Railroad Journal* will be printed on a sheet of the largest size (mammoth), and put up in a convenient form for binding, each number to sixteen large octavo pages of three columns each. The selections, upon the subject of railroads and other works of internal improvement will be from the best authors, both of Europe and America, and will be occasionally illustrated by engravings. A part of this Journal will be devoted to the subject of internal improvement — giving a history of the first introduction of railroads into England and their improvement to the present day. It will also notice the meetings, in different sections of the country, upon the subject of railroads. The remaining part of the paper will contain the Literary, Miscellaneous and News matter of the *New York American*, as prepared for that paper, omitting all political subjects, except such as are of general interest."

AMERICAN RAILROAD JOURNAL,
AND ADVOCATE OF INTERNAL IMPROVEMENTS

PUBLISHED WEEKLY, AT NO. 132 NASSAU STREET, NEW-YORK, AT FIVE DOLLARS PER ANNUM, PAYABLE IN ADVANCE.

D. K. MINOR, Editor.]   SATURDAY, MARCH 26, 1836.   [VOLUME V.—No. 13.

The first issue contained a printer's fluke, according to Harry L. Eddy, Librarian, Association of American Railroads. By error, the compositor set the official publication date as January 2, 1831 in the heading. The new Journal was locked-up in the chase, placed on the press and proofs run. All day the pressmen rolled out copies of the new railroad publication. Much to the disgust of D. K. Minor, editor of the Journal, the mistake in publication date of the year previous was noticed after a few copies were released to a selected group of railroad men, financiers and dignitaries. All available copies were destroyed, the date corrected to January 1, 1832, and the forms returned to the press. The Association of American Railroads have the only known copies of the first edition showing the dual publication dates.

While the *Railroad Advocate* was the first railroad publication in this country, the readership of the *American Railroad Journal* continued to grow. The Journal offered general news such as incorporations, openings of lines, and occasionally notes on locomotives and car builders. H. V. Poor was soon to replace D. K. Minor as editor, and the Journal changed its format to the financial side of the new railroad industry. The name *American Railroad Journal* was changed in favor of *Railroad & Engineering Journal* in 1887 when M. N. Forney took control of the publication. Forney's *The Catechism of the Locomotive* made him famous and an expert in the field of locomotive construction. Within a short time mechanics and engineering matters were the main topics discussed in the weekly Journal. After 1893 the magazine went through several title changes and finally suspended in 1938.

The yellowing pages of the old *American Railroad Journal* offer the historian the knowledge of our earliest railroad lines. For a publication of such wide circulation only three institutions in the United States possess a complete file. They are the Franklin Institute (Philadelphia), Library of Congress and the Association of American Railroads (Washington, D.C.). Before long this time-honored publication will be lost to the ages. ❖❖❖

RAIL-ROAD JOURNAL.

VOL. I.   NEW-YORK, JANUARY 2, 1831. (2.)   NO. 1.

The first issue of the *American Railroad Journal* contained a printer's fluke. The compositor inadvertently set the publication date as January 2, 1831, in the heading. A reproduction of this error is shown above, while below, the same issue with the correct date of January 2, 1832. (*Upper Left*) The masthead as it appeared during the fifth year. Note the carriage loaded on the flat car, which might well have been the first application of our so-called modern "piggyback."—ASSOCIATION OF AMERICAN RAILROADS

RAIL-ROAD JOURNAL.

VOL. I.   NEW-YORK, JANUARY 2, 1832.   NO. 1.

Driving Wheels (Southern Pacific No. 3025)—*Donald Duke*

Table of Contents

Preface - 5

Amcrican Railroad Journal — 1832 - - - - - - - - - - 6

The Locomotive Engineer — *by Donald Duke* - - - - - - 10

Two-Eight-Eight-Four — *by Roger Valentine* - - - - - - 23

Railroaders' Lingo — *compiled by Freeman Hubbard* - - - 35

Last of the Birneys — *by E. S. Peyton and R. A. Moorman* - 66

America's First Main Line Electrification — *by Donald Duke* - 87

The Single Drivered Steam Locomotive in the West —
    by Gerald M. Best - - - - - - - - - - - - - - 110

Index - 119

The Locomotive Engineer

by Donald Duke

Ever since the first fire was kindled beneath a steam locomotive boiler, the engineer has been the symbol of all railroad men. "Perhaps no other occupation," says Lucius Beebe, "ever fetched the American fancy as did that of the locomotive engineer. Not even the cowboy, the Indian scout, the godlike vision of Washington at Valley Forge or the swift facility of 'Tinker to Evers to Chance' quite so effectively captivate the national imagination as the steam locomotive, its drive-rods flashing obedient to the crossheads in their guides and the dynamic whole obedient to the visor-capped man at the throttle. His eagle eye pierced the impenetrable storm and saw to the farthest horizons; his controlling hand on the air brake was the hand of fate itself." The friendly wave of the engineer and the chromatic tones of the steam whistle offered irresistible invitations to the many venturesome boys who hungered for something more challenging than a tedious life behind the plow.

In the pantheon of American rail heroes, the throttle artist assigned to Pennsylvania Railroad's *Broadway Limited* was the envy of the road. This high roller dressed in the uniform of his calling, glances down the trim K-4 Pacific type 4-6-2 as he watches the color signals swimming in the distance.—H. ARMSTRONG ROBERTS

The first locomotive engineers were the inventors and builders of the machines. They were practical men and knew the temperament of the boilers they built. As the demand for engineers increased it became customary to select the engine drivers among machinists. *The Monthly Journal* for September 1868 noted: "There was a time before railroads were regarded as a permanent institution of the country, when engineers were required to be thorough in their profession, both practically and theoretically; and they were recommended according to their merits." The belief that only machinists could run a steam locomotive quickly changed, partly as a result of the demand for engineers, which could not be met from the ranks of the trade alone, and the knowledge that mechanical ability was not always a substitute for experience.

The engineer was often elected by the Board of Directors of many early day American railroads. The man at the throttle then in turn hired his own fireman and assumed his wages. On the Erie Railroad, for instance, there was always a test of strength between the engineer and conductor to choose the "master" of the train. Years later, the conductor was officially selected to assume the role of "captain" of the caravan of steam cars. There were many curious practices during the early years of railroading, although operating procedures were soon standardized. The official Book of Rules became the railroaders' bible.

The conditions surrounding the engineer's life on the rail has greatly changed today. Way back when, the engineer had no cab but stood on a little open platform connecting the engine with tender. He took the weather as it came, sheltering his eyes with pieces of firewood during a severe storm. The cab was not generally adopted until 1850, and why this took so long to occur, one can never imagine. By this time the engineer had come a long way.

When a train highballed out of the station in the old days the engineer was on his own, a man who rode destiny and twisted her tail. The book *Wonders and Curiosities of the Railway* published in 1874 had this to say: "The life of an engineer is not an enviable one. Apart from the wearing sense of responsibility, there is the strain and jar received by the nervous system." The thrill of leaning out the right-hand side of the cab window, and whistling an arrogant toot to the girls at the crossing presented a gallant adventure. It overruled the strain on body and nervous system with the result that many a man risked everything for a good life on the high iron.

For many years, engineers in company service were assigned to a regular engine more or less permanently. The "runner" as most engineers were called, considered the locomotive his own iron horse and took personal interest in the beast. The behemoth of iron and steel became a human being with life and intelligence and the driver cared for its every mood. The cab was often a sort of second home for the engineer and his fireboy. Together they polished the glittering brass as did the character in "Pinafore" who "polished up the handle on the big front door". The locomotive was the engineer's pride and joy and never was there a lover more jealous of his sweetheart than an engineer for his engine.

When not on a regular run many hours were spent at hard labor keeping the machine in topnotch repair. You were not considered to be a good "runner" if you sent your steed into the roundhouse too often for repair. The fewer defects reported, the better standing you had with the roundhouse foreman and the general manager. There was always a chance you might be the next one in line for promotion if you had a smooth running locomotive. It was quite natural enginemen should take a deep interest in their locomotives; many of

Way back when, the locomotive engineer had no cab but stood on a little platform connecting the engine with tender. This silhouette of the celebrated *De Witt Clinton* and two coaches was drawn on the spot.—Connecticut Historical Society

the fittings were adjusted to their individual liking.

Back in the halcyon era many a locomotive had a whistle of the engineer's own manufacture, a steam whistle with a distinctive musical tone. The technique of blowing this whistle was called "quilling". Many on the railroad could tell the engineer's name the moment his whistle was heard. Casey Jones was the classic example of a "ballast scorcher" with a melodious quill whistle. As the song relates,

"The switchmen knew by the engine's moan

That the man at the throttle was Casey Jones."

"Engineer Jones had a six-chime whistle," according to Freeman Hubbard's book *Railroad Avenue.* "It was formed by six slender tubes banded together, the shortest exactly half the length of the tallest. With its interpretive tone the ballast scorcher could make that quill say its prayers or scream like a banshee."

As steel rails pushed across America the railroads soon learned that full motive power utilization was not being obtained under the permanent assignment system. On many of the larger roads the "first in — first out" method was adopted. This meant the engines were assigned in the order in which they came in from a run. The engineer took whatever machine happened to fall to his lot. Consternation prevailed among the engineers, but protests were made without avail. The personal touch to American railroading had come to the end of the line.

The greatest concern of the engineer was to "make time". Many of the 19th century trains were so scheduled that the engineer had to keep his locomotive up to the highest efficiency to reach the destination on time. A little carelessness in firing, the letting of cold water into the boiler irregularly or slackening more than was necessary might cause a delay in arrival at the terminus. Railroad men were religious about keeping trains "on time".

The locomotive engineer was the popular hero of the day for more than 50 years. *Frank Leslie's Illustrated Newspaper* often carried articles about the brave men who took chances and gave their lives to save the train. Many a dime thriller pictured the engineer out on the cow-catcher, clinging with one hand, while the other was outstretched to save Polly from the churning wheels of the onrushing horse of iron. In the early days the engine was the most dangerous part of the railroad. The engineer was subject to boiler explosions and mechanical breakdowns which often threw his machine into the ditch. The engineer true to his calling was often a real hero, and many lives were saved by his quick-witted actions.

The railroad nurtured a special breed of courage. Men who took chances and gave their lives to save the train and passengers. Here are two classic examples of heroism from the pages of *Harper's Weekly.* (*Above*) At the brink of danger, the train is saved by the quick action of the engineer and his fireboy. (*Below*) "There was no time to think. In a few seconds Jim was out on the cow-catcher, clinging by one hand. The other outstretched toward Polly."

On a frenzied winter's night, a glimpse of cab life aboard the mighty steam locomotive. (*Left*) The station platform lights of Sherbrooke, Quebec, penetrate the darkness as a Canadian National hogger leaves his warm cab for an inspection of the locomotive. Although a blanket of snow marks its departure, the "Night Train" will arrive on time. — BOTH JIM SHAUGHNESSY

This old engraving represents the cab end of a New York Central & Hudson River Railroad steam locomotive, circa 1880. While the engineer of this generation had his hands full, the operation of this vintage engine was kindergarten compared with the manipulations required to handle the rail giants of our time.—Donald Duke Collection

1. Engine bell rope.

2. Train bell rope.

3. Train bell or gong.

4. Lever for blowing whistle.

5. Steam gauge to indicate pressure in boiler.

6. Steam gauge lamp to illuminate face of gauge.

7. Pressure gauge for air brake; to show pressure in air reservoirs.

8. Valve to admit steam to air brake pump.

9. Automatic lubricator for oiling main valves.

10. Cock for admitting steam to lubricator.

11. Handle for opening valves in sandbox to sand the rails.

12. Handle for opening the cocks which drain the water from the cylinders.

13. Valve for admitting steam to the jets which force air into the firebox.

14. Throttle valve lever. This is for opening the valve which admits steam to the cylinders.

15. Sector by which the throttle lever is held in any desired position.

16. "Lazy-cock" handle. A valve which regulates the water supply to the pumps and is worked by this handle.

17. Reverse lever.

18. Reverse lever sector.

19. Gauge cocks for showing the height of the water in the boiler. 19'. is a pipe for carrying away the water which escapes when the gauge cocks are opened.

20. Oil cups for oiling the cylinders.

21. Handle for working steam valve of injector.

22. Handle for controlling water-jet of the injector.

23. Handle for working water valve of injector.

24. Oil can shelf.

25. Handle for air brake valve.

26. Valve for controlling air brake.

27. Pipe for conducting air to brakes under the cars.

28. Pipe connected with air reservoir.

29. Pipe connection to air pump.

30. Handle for working a valve which admits or shuts off the air for the driving wheel brakes.

31. Valve for driving wheel brakes.

32. Lever for moving a diaphragm in smokebox by which the draught is regulated.

33. Handle for raising or lowering snow scrapers in front of truck wheels.

34. Handle for opening cock on pump to show whether it is forcing water into the boiler.

35. Lamp to light the water gauge.

36. Air hole for admitting air to firebox.

37. Tallow can for oiling cylinders.

38. Oil can.

39. Shelf for warming oil cans.

40. Firebox door.

41. Chain for opening and closing firebox door.

42. Handles for opening dampers on the ash pan.

43. Lubricators for air pump.

44. Valve for admitting steam to the chimney to blow the fire when the engine is standing still.

45. Valve for admitting steam to the train pipes for warming the cars.

46. Valve for reducing the pressure of the steam used for heating cars.

47. Cock which admits steam to the pressure gauge.

48. Pressure gauge which indicates the steam pressure in heater pipes.

49. Pipe for conducting steam to the train to heat the cars.

50. Cock for water gauge.

51. Glass water gauge to indicate the height of water in the boiler.

52. Cock for blowing off impurities from the surface of the water in the boiler.

The engineer laid his hand upon the throttle lever and it trembled slightly—as well it might; the huge iron horse quivered and stiffened as it braced itself for the task ahead. Noisily and imperceptibly the steam locomotive moved ahead, expelling one mighty breath, then another and another, until its respirations were lost in one continuous flow of steam.—Library of Congress

Early locomotives were personalities in their own right. They bore interesting names like "Pioneer", "Tiger", and "The Prairie King". "An engine to a boy of my time," wrote an old engineer, "was not a machine at all, but a living animal, perhaps some species of mastodon, in any case an animal that had lungs and could breathe." Steam locomotives, so far as their mechanical construction was concerned, looked similar; some were larger than others, but each machine had an individuality of its own. It was rare that two locomotives were alike, even when turned out at the locomotive works the very same day. To the man at the throttle, "no engine was worth a plugged-nickel unless it could steam." Not every engine was a good steamer, but a great deal of science was required by the fireman who shoveled the coal into the firebox. A good fireboy knew his engine and the right spot to place the coal in order to produce a boiler full of steam. The engineer likewise had to know how to use this steam to obtain maximum efficiency from the locomotive.

By the time a fireman had worked behind a shovel for several years he knew every part of the locomotive and the transition from fireman to engineer became general practice. For the adventurous lad who achieved his dream of becoming an engineer, a new and somewhat challenging life opened up for him. Railroading flowed through his veins, yet the road to the right-hand side was not always easy and swift. Cy Warman, one of the greatest railroad fiction writers of all time, moved from cornfield to throttle. Warman had a good life on the old narrow gauge Denver & Rio Grande, and we quote from his book *Tales of An Engineer* published in 1895:

"First I joined the wipers, — a gang of half a dozen men, whose business it was to clean the engines when they came in from the road. This gang was made up of three classes, — old men who were not strong enough to perform heavier work; young and delicate youths; strong young men who expected to become firemen when their names were reached.

"Before long, the foreman, if he thought you deserved to be encouraged, put you on a yard engine as fireman. This took you one step forward. From the yard engine you went out on the road, and then you were a real fireman. You were assigned a regular locomotive, and expected to keep everything clean and in order; that is, everything above the running board, — that board extending from the cab along the side of the boiler to the front end.

"At the end, say, of three years, the fireman might be promoted to hostler. The hostler took the engines from the coal-track, side-track, or wherever

The locomotive engineer signs in at the roundhouse office, then checks the assignment sheets for a listing of his engine and name of the fireman for the day.—SANTA FE RAILWAY (*Below*) The engineer starts his usual inspection, carefully noting the condition of the running gear, seeing the automatic lubricators are full, and oiling the moving parts.—WILLIAM D. MIDDLETON

Backhead of a modern steam locomotive with its jungle of valves, handles, gauges and pipes. The automatic stoker may be seen in the center as it emerges from the cab floor.—PITTSBURGH & LAKE ERIE RAILROAD (*Below*) Highball! The Engineer shoves the reverse lever forward, then opens the throttle with his left hand. — SANTA FE RAILWAY (*Lower Right*) The engineer and conductor pore over their watches to be sure each timepiece is correct to the second.—SOUTHERN PACIFIC

the engineers left them. He had them coaled up, the fire cleaned, and then run into the stalls of the roundhouse. In this work the hostler became familiar with each and every engine on the division, and if he be observing, he would retain this knowledge and use it when he became an engineer.

"The next promotion took the hostler back to the yard engine, this time as engineer. The man on the yard engine went through the same stages of promotion that the fireman went through, until at last he found himself at the throttle of a road engine."

Many a locomotive engineer rushed toward the twentieth century likely as not behind the throttle of a little thoroughbred styled American in the locomotive classification manuals. In wheel arrangement it was 4-4-0, with big drivers, tall smokestacks, and simple valve gear. A new breed of motive power loomed over the horizon, machines which were bigger, faster, more flexible and efficient. Such changes revolutionized the railroad, just as the invention and application of the first air brake did.

In all its smoking glory this new horse of iron was equipped with steel castings, wide fireboxes, roller bearings, superheaters, boosters and automatic stokers. Instead of working the scoop, the fireman now operated a knob which controlled an automatic stoker which brought coal from tender to firebox by means of a screw conveyor. In many

Nearly every adventurous lad dreamed of the day when he might don a visored cap and guide the destinies of the steam locomotive.—DONALD DUKE

(*Left*) This photograph of a locomotive engineer and a small boy is without doubt the most widely circulated railroad portrait ever published. It appeared in over five million copies of the *Quiz on Railroads and Railroading* issued by the Association of American Railroads and photo prints were requested around-the-world. This picture first appeared on the cover of the February 1938, issue of the *Southern Pacific Bulletin* with this explanation: "This time of year young railroaders have serious problems. Trains that ran smoothly at Christmas time now need heavy repairs. Faced with this plight, little Donald, son of Leo J. Lyons, superintendent of freight car service for Southern Pacific, called on Billy Jones, locomotive engineer at Mission Bay roundhouse, San Francisco, for a consultation. At last report, the two managed to put the railroad back on its feet."—SOUTHERN PACIFIC

regions of America oil became the prime fuel for this new breed of steam locomotive. The cab still had the same essential controls, but had grown and changed beyond recognition. The modern engineer had at his fingertips new levers, handles and knobs which could start, stop and control 500 tons of traveling power.

Hallmark of all steam locomotives appeared in 1941 when Union Pacific's 4-8-8-4 single-expansion articulated steam locomotives called "Big Boy" hit the high iron. They were a battling steel leviathan weighing over a million pounds. What a marvelous and unforgettable sight it was to watch this, the world's mightiest locomotive cope with Sherman Hill of southern Wyoming.

Far down the line of single track the signals in front of the steam locomotive switched to yellow — then red. The diesel in its variegated paint job rushed into the second half of the twentieth century to demean the stature of the engineer and the wonderments of his time-honored machine. True, the diesel could pack more weight per axle, didn't chew up the rails, required fewer trips to the repair shop, and saved fuel bills. Those who loved the reciprocating steam locomotive also found the aroma of hot steam and oil smoke pleasing, and the malodorous smell of the throbbing diesel most distasteful. No matter how one looked at this colorful centipede on railroad wheels, it wasn't an iron horse as we know it — or knew it.

As long as flanged wheels pound on steel rails there will be locomotive engineers. The Casey Jones of today is really no more than a motorman behind an internal combustion machine. The prow of the diesel extending forward from the windshield resembles the hood of an automobile and the seats inside the cab are upholstered. The polished levers and knobs of the steamer have been replaced by a dashboard full of push-buttons, gauges and dials. The throttle looks more like the controller on an old time trolley.

The boy on top the hill who waved at the friendly engineer now looks toward the skies and imitates the sound of jet engines. The era of the steam locomotive and the tales of brave engineers sleep as Americana on the printed page. Before taking the final run to the other side of Jordan, many an old retired engineer would like to place his hand once more on the big throttle and feel the quiver of live steam.

Out of the fond and glorious age of the steam locomotive, the engineer in his visored cab behind the hurricane of power was "King of the Rails". He was the overlord of the loud, dirty, hot, pounding world of banging metal, smoke and steam. We shall never see their like again. ✧✧✧

Extra No. 3811 with a firebox of hot coals thunders a westbound 100-car freight drag between Tucumcari, New Mexico, and El Paso, Texas. — R. H. KINDIG

TWO-EIGHT-EIGHT-FOUR

by Roger Valentine

LONG BEFORE WORLD WAR II, the Southern Pacific in common with other railroads of the United States, felt the stress of rising operating costs. To meet these conditions, the locomotive builders were asked to design a more efficient steam locomotive, an engine that would be capable of hauling heavier loads at faster speeds while offering fuel and maintenance savings.

The first major step in the modernization of Southern Pacific's motive power was the arrival in 1936 of six fast passenger locomotives. These famous Lima-built *Daylight* type 4-8-4 locomotives were streamlined and dressed in red, orange, and black livery. They were the for-runners of a renowned fleet of modern passenger locomotives. During this same period, the Baldwin Locomotive Works were improving the design of the familiar "Cab-In-Front" articulated which was used in heavy freight and passenger service.

Around-the-world the Cab-Aheads were tagged "Mister Espee". True, they were certainly a departure from the accepted construction of articulated locomotives. Over the years, the Southern Pacific roster included many other interesting classes of Mallets. In 1939 the Lima Locomotive Works delivered 12 modern 2-8-8-4 Super-Power coal-burning, semi-streamlined steam locomotives for use in the Southwest. These engines were just as unconventional on Southern Pacific during their 16-year reign as a "Cab-In-Front" might have appeared on the rails of the Pennsylvania Railroad. The story of these 12 locomotives and the development of the Mallet in the United States is worthy of comment.

The rapidly growing freight density of 50 years ago created a demand for steam locomotives of greater hauling capacity. To boost the power of a locomotive involved an increase in the number of driving wheels, the weight on the drivers, larger cylinders, higher steam pressure, heavier pistons and other reciprocating parts. The increase of all these items only created another problem for the American railroad official. If such a locomotive were built it would then be necesary to restrict the length of the rigid wheel base to suit existing track. Then if high speed was to be maintained, the weight on each driving wheel would have to be kept within safe limits, otherwise the wheels could not be counterbalanced. They were back at the start of the problem.

The Mallet locomotive which originated in France seemed to offer the solution to the problem. The driving wheels on the Mallet were divided into two groups, each held by separate frames and connected by a hinge joint. The boiler was rigidly attached to the rear frame and supported on the front frame by a sliding bearing. Compound cylinders were used, the high-pressure pair driving the rear group of wheels, the low pressure pair furnishing the power for the forward group of wheels. This arrangement made it possible to build a locomotive with 12, 16, or 20 pairs of driving wheels under one boiler.

The first Mallet in the United States was built in 1904 for the Baltimore & Ohio Railroad. While the Mallet showed economy in fuel and water consumption at slow speeds, it had many inherent disadvantages. First, the heavy reciprocating parts increased maintenance costs. The high back-pressure on the low pressure pistons resulted in a very unequal division of power, plus the difficulty in developing starting tractive force up to the limits of adhesion. Most important, the Mallet was unsuitable for fast road speeds.

In order to retain the hauling capacity and economy of the Mallet locomotive and at the same time overcome its many disadvantages, the single-expansion articulated locomotive was developed. This type of locomotive retained the articulated feature of the Mallet, but used high-pressure steam in all four cylinders which were of the same size.

Baltimore & Ohio No. 2400 affectionately called "Old Maude" was the first mallet built in America. This 0-6-6-0 type locomotive looked small compared to the enormous 3800 class. — SMITHSONIAN INSTITUTION

With this arrangement the maximum locomotive width was kept within reasonable limits, the back-pressure lowered, and the speed greatly increased. With superheated steam, the four-cylinder, single-expansion locomotive showed an economy comparable to that of the Mallet, except possibly at slow drag speeds.

As traffic increased, railroads required a superior single-expansion articulated locomotive with even higher speeds and better fuel consumptioin to meet rising costs without exceeding existing wheel load and clearance limits. It was obvious that higher speeds necessitated larger boiler capacity, which in turn demanded larger grate areas to avoid an excessive fuel rate. Also, higher speeds would increase the stress on track structures, unless a new design could possess the desired high horsepower, without extending the limits of axle loads. This combination of requirements pointed to a redistribution of locomotive weight and the use of a 4-wheel trailing truck.

In 1925 a new design was introduced when the Lima Locomotive Works announced its experimental locomotive known as "A-1". In addition to the 4-wheel trailing truck, this experimental locomotive included many new innovations in design which were later accepted as standard practice. Included among these were higher boiler pressure, cast steel cylinders for weight saving, a Type E superheater and the locomotive booster. Following the great success of Lima's "A-1",

several hundred steam locomotives, based substantially on this design, were built for American railroads. This design became known as the Lima Super-Power locomotive, and its objectives were maximum power output per driving axle; the most economical use of steam in the cylinders under all conditions of service; and a boiler with a fire-box capable of supplying abundant steam at high efficiency.

The Southern Pacific received 12 of these 2-8-8-4 Super-Power coal-burning articulated passenger and freight locomotives from the Lima Locomotive Works during the latter part of 1939. They were the longest and heaviest pieces of motive power on the entire Southern Pacific system. The locomotives were designed for the Rio Grande Division and placed in service between El Paso, Texas, and Tucumcari, New Mexico, a distance of 332 miles. This trackage had mountain grades reaching a maximum elevation of 6,724 feet and ascending grades of one per cent. The line rises 3,000 feet eastbound from El Paso to the summit between Gallina and Corona, New Mexico, and 2,700 feet westbound between Tucumcari and the summit.

It might seem strange that so modern a steam locomotive in the West would be built as a coal burner when the majority of all Southern Pacific power burned oil. These 12 Super-Power locomotives were designed to burn the low grade bituminous coal from the Dawson Field in New Mex-

In the latter part of 1939 Lima Locomotive Works delivered 12 "Super Power" 2-8-8-4 articulated steam locomotives to the Southern Pacific. They were the longest and heaviest pieces of motive power on the railroad. In the view above, a portrait of No. 3800 at the Lima Locomotive Works prior to delivery. *(Left)* Front view of the behemoth with its massive air pumps and solid steel pilot. — Both Southern Pacific Collection

SPECIFICATIONS

Built for
Southern Pacific Lines

Class: 2-8-8-4-S-689.9   R. R. Class: AC-9   Road No. 3800

Order Covers 12 Locos. 3800–3811

GAUGE OF TRACK	DRIVING WHEEL DIAMETER	FUEL Kind	CYLINDERS Diameter	Stroke	BOILER Diameter	Pressure	FIREBOX Length	Width
4'-8½"	63½"	Soft Coal	24"	32"	109⅛"	250 Lbs.	205²¹⁄₃₂"	102¼"

Driving	WHEEL BASE Engine	Engine and Tender	TRACTIVE POWER Main Cylinders	FACTOR OF ADHESION	TUBES & FLUES Number	Diameter	Length
44'-7"	66'-3"	112'-11⅞"	124300	4.27	86	2¼"	22'-0"
					260	3½"	

AVERAGE WEIGHT IN WORKING ORDER, Pounds						GRATE AREA Sq. Ft.	HEATING SURFACES, Square Feet				
On Drivers	Truck	Trailer Front Axle	Rear Axle	Total Engine	Tender ⅔ Load		Tubes & Flues	Circulators	Firebox & Comb. Cham.	Total	Superheater
531200	48300	48900	61500	689900	320700	139.3	6329	124	465	6918	2831

TENDER, TYPE 12 WHEEL   CAPACITY, WATER 22120 GALLONS   FUEL, 28 TONS

LIMA
LOCOMOTIVE WORKS
INCORPORATED

ico because the coal was plentiful, cheap, and provided a heating value of approximately 1,200 B.t.u. per pound. However during 1950, with 100 per cent dieselization of the Rio Grande Division in the offing, these engines were converted to oil and later transferred to Northern California and Nevada on a line without tunnels.

The Southern Pacific gave this 2-8-8-4 design the road classification of AC-9 with numbering in the 3800 series. The letters AC stood for "Articulated Consolidation" and were ninth in a series of similar type locomotives; the remaining AC groups were of the "Cab-In-Front" design.

Without extensive application of extra sheathing as used on the famous *Daylight* 4-8-4's, the 3800's were semi-streamlined. They had a clean and pleasing appearance by the application of the "skyline" casing over the top of the boiler and a decorative reinforced steel plate pilot. The boiler and cab were conical in shape lending to a more streamlined appearance than the conventional articulated locomotive. Number 3800 was the first locomotive of the series shipped West by Lima, and it is claimed that this number was striped in orange and white similar to the *Daylight* design, though this paint scheme was not carried out on the balance of the order.

Each locomotive had a total weight of 689,000 pounds, of which 77 per cent was on drivers, and it developed a rated tractive force of 124,300

pounds. The boiler carried a working pressure of 250 pounds per square inch, and the cylinders had a 24-inch diameter by 32-inch stroke. The diameter of the driving wheels was 63½ inches, thus permitting speeds of 75 miles per hour on level track, plus an ability to negotiate curves up to 18 degrees.

The AC-9's were much the same in capacity and general construction as the "Cab-In-Front" type which had been used all over the Southern Pacific system since 1928. The only actual distinction was the placement of the cab behind the boiler. On a coal burning locomotive, the boiler had to be in direct line with the fuel source. The boilers of the 3800's were slightly larger than the "Cab-In-Front" type and more conical in shape.

The firebox was nearly 206 inches in length inside the mud rings, and of welded construction, with the exception of the tube sheet which was riveted in the combustion chamber. Six Nathan boiler drop plugs were placed in the crown sheet of the combustion chamber to prevent a boiler explosion caused by overheating due to low water.

Through the desolate beauty of New Mexico, Southern Pacific fast iron stretches between Tucumcari, New Mexico, and El Paso, Texas. In the scene below, No. 3811 stirs the desert air west of Hargis, New Mexico. — R. H. KINDIG

The firebox was of the Firebar type and coal was fed by a standard MB type stoker with the engine on the left side of the tender. All of this equipment was removed when the conversion was made to oil burning. The boiler feeding equipment comprised a Nathan No. 17 Simplex injector and a Hancock exhaust-steam turbo feedwater heater. The turbo feedwater heater was mounted below the cab on the left side and could deliver 13,000 gallons of water to the boiler per hour.

The foundation of each of the locomotive units was a Commonwealth bed casting in which the cylinders were integrally cast. The cylinder spread was 93 inches, and the second barrel course of the boiler was carried on the rear cylinder saddle. The rear of the firebox was carried on oil lubricated expansion shoes.

The hinged radius bar at the rear of the front bed casting pivoted about a 7-inch ball joint pocketed in the rear cylinder saddle. The driving journal boxes were of the crown bearing type with spring-pad oil lubricators in special cellars which were developed by the Southern Pacific at their Sacramento Shops. Supplementing the spring-pad lubricator, oil was fed to the journals from a force-fed mechanical lubricator.

Steam for both engine units left the front-end branch pipes through a single pair of outside steam pipes, one on each side of the locomotive. Each of these pipes was nine inches in diameter and carried back from the elbow casting at the side of the smoke box to the front of the rear cylinders where there was a slip joint connection. Live steam for the front pair of cylinders was carried forward from the front face of the rear saddle casting by a single eight-inch pipe on the longitudinal center line of the locomotive. Exhaust pipes from the rear cylinders extended forward along each side of the locomotive toward the smokebox. At the smokebox end the exhaust pipe flange was bolted to the smokebox elbow connection. The flexible exhaust pipe from the front cylinders were made up of two sections of cast iron pipe which joined by a long slip joint. Steam distribution was effected by the Walschaert valve motion which drove an 11-inch valve with maximum travel of six and one-half inches. Alco Type H reverse gear was included.

Tucumcari, New Mexico, end of the line for Southern Pacific rails. Here the Rock Island throttles eastbound traffic over the famous "Golden State Route". In the scene above, No. 3804 waits on the ready track at the engine terminal and yard. — L. E. GRIFFITHS *(Left)* At full throttle, a freight leaves El Paso in a mist of hot steam and smoke. — STAN KISTLER COLLECTION *(Opposite Page)* Under a cloud of black smoke a freight sweeps across the New Mexico countryside at 40 on the speed indicator. — R. H. KINDIG *(Below)* With a clear track all the way to El Paso, No. 3810 chugs a stack full of black smoke as it leaves Tucumcari. — R. H. KINDIG

The main driving axle was the third on each engine unit. The side rods had fixed bronze crankpin bearings on the first and fourth pairs of driving wheels, and floating bushings on the main and intermediate crank pins. The back end of the main rod also had a floating bushing bearing. The guides and crosshead were of the multiple-bearing type. The crossheads were cast steel with bronze rings inside to prevent galling of the front end of the main rod. The pistons were of light alloy steel with combination bronze and iron packing rings. Main and side rods, driving axles, engine and trailer-truck axles, crank pins were of normalized and drawn carbon steel.

The lubrication system, so important on any locomotive, was of the finest construction. There were four force-feed mechanical lubricators on each locomotive, two for journal box oil and two for valve oil. One of these was placed on the left side of each locomotive where it could be driven from the link by the valve motion. All crank pins, eccentric crank pins and rods were internally pressure lubricated.

The steel cab was of the closed vestibule type and completely insulated to protect crews from the cold New Mexico wind. The cab interior contained a large working area and a seat and window for the head brakeman on the rear left side. There was a turret for both superheated and saturated steam. The superheated steam section of the turret served the blower, stoker, stoker engine, stoker jets and soot blower. An auxiliary turret on the left side of the smokebox supplied superheated steam to the air compressors and steam whistle. Each locomotive contained an air horn mounted high on the right side of the "skyline" casing in addition to the steam whistle. This was common practice on all modern Southern Pacific steam power. The blast from the air horn was more powerful and could be heard more distinctly at closer range than the steam whistle. The air brake equipment was of Westinghouse manufacture and two cross compound compressors were mounted on the smokebox front.

The driving tires and tender wheels were provided with an air controlled water cooling system which had been developed by the Southern Pacific. This unique wheel cooling system operated automatically whenever brakes were applied. As the engineer applied his brakes, he also opened a control valve on the wheel cooling system causing a sufficient amount of water to flow on the wheels to counteract the heating effect of the brake shoes.

The gigantic tender held 28 tons of coal and 22,210 gallons of water, enough to fill several large size swimming pools. *(Below)* The steel cab was of the closed vestibule type in order to protect crews from the New Mexico wind. — BOTH GUY L. DUNSCOMB

With the complete dieselization of the Rio Grande Division in 1953, the 3800's worked their way west to Alturas located in the upper portion of California. *(Above)* The crack streamliner "San Joaquin Daylight" waits in a siding while No. 3809 rumbles a fast freight up the valley. *(Right)* Farther up the line, the same freight slows down for the many city crossings which plague the Southern Pacific at Turlock. — BOTH GUY L. DUNSCOMB

For almost two years the 3800's provided helper service on the "Modoc" line running down the eastern slopes of the Sierra Nevadas between Alturas, California, and Fernley, Nevada. *(Above)* A mile-long freight curls itself around the parched foothills of the Smoke Creek Desert after passing the nearly dry Pyramid Lake. — GUY L. DUNSCOMB *(Upper left)* No. 3808 glides down the bottom leg of the Likely "S" grade. — RICHARD STEINHEIMER *(Left)* The rhythm of crossheads and reciprocating side-rods blends with stack talk as No. 3808 shoves a drag freight west through Likely, California. — JOHN SHAW *(Below)* Rail excursion on the "Modoc" line in 1954. — GUY L. DUNSCOMB *(Upper right)* After all the others were scrapped, No. 3804, the last survivor of its class, meets a "Cab-in-Front" on a helper run at Ravondale. — RICHARD STEINHEIMER

The tender had a 28-ton coal capacity and water capacity of 22,120 gallons. Each tender was built upon a General Steel Casting underframe and carried on two buckeye six-wheel trucks. The conversion from coal to oil was made at the El Paso shops in 1950.

With the complete dieselization of the Rio Grande Division in the spring of 1953, the 3800's worked their way west to Los Angeles. They climbed Tehachapi and rolled up the San Joaquin Valley to Sacramento, then north to Klamath Falls, Oregon, before dropping down to Alturas. This strange route was designed to avoid the close clearances of the Donner Pass snow sheds.

For almost two years, the 3800's provided a connection with the main east-west line and helper service on the "Modoc" line which runs from Alturas, California, down the east side of the Sierras to Fernley, Nevada. Quite often the 3800's ran directly into Sparks, Nevada, the main home base for east-west and north-south motive power.

Number 3800 was the first of the series to be scrapped and never came west from El Paso. As each locomotive unit came due for major overhaul, it was singled out and slated for scrapping.

At various intervals through 1955, the balance of the 11 locomotives finally fell to their betters.

The end of steam on the Rio Grande Division brought about the eventual closing of the coal mines at Dawson. The Dawson branch, approximately 18 miles of line, ran north from the Santa Fe main line at French to the Dawson Coal Field. This was taken up. All that remains is the direct 132 mile connection from Tucumcari to the Santa Fe main at French, a line across rolling barren land.

Not much remains of Dawson, nor the quaint coal burning 3400 class 2-8-0 type locomotives which were the mainstay of the branch till the bitter end. Gone are the coaling facilities along the Tucumcari - El Paso main stem which heard the familiar echo of the 3800's as they rolled along the desert grade of New Mexico.

In the final analysis the 12 semi-streamlined articulated Super-Power locomotives proved their worth. They demonstrated a direct saving in operations by their increased hauling capacity. They were short lived as steam locomotives go and only the more advanced capabilities of the diesel age brought about their demise. ✦✦✦

Railroaders' Lingo

compiled by Freeman Hubbard

BACK IN THE nineteenth century, when railroads were the prime means of transportation, nearly every population center, large or small, was linked by the iron rail. The depot, that may have stood at the foot of Main Street or anywhere else, became the social center of town, and the station agent a highly respected member of the community. That was the Golden Era, when a career on the roaring road was a pathway to adventure. Many a lad trudging home from school took to the tracks and walked the rails leading to the depot. Bug-eyed and all ears, he listened to the chatter of Morse and the wild tales of the bespectacled old operator. Almost every farm boy dreamed of the day when he would kick the cow and go firin' or brakin', and talk like a railroad man.

In the days before radio and motion pictures, there wasn't much to do after the day's work was done. Once *Frank Leslie's Illustrated Weekly* had been digested, the railroad men would gather around the big red-bellied stove at the roundhouse or station or crew room and talk shop. Here stories were told of great deeds and life on the "high iron," and these conversations developed new words. A man related his experiences in slang, just as a cowboy's thoughts ran to sentimental song. The railroader's occupation was reflected in his language. Such jargon, like that of the lumberjack or journalist, has enriched our common tongue and blended with it to such an extent that only a lexicographer can tell which terms have been accepted and which have not. It has often been stated that yesterday's slang is today's academic English.

In the modern world of diesel locomotives, electronic switch yards, and radio dispatching, the picturesque old terms of railroad men are no longer part of our vocabulary. Many look down their noses at such words, of which they don't even know the meaning. This thesaurus records a body of rail lingo before it is lost to the ages. I began it in 1932 when I compiled my first glossary for the magazine then called *Railroad Stories*. From that rather fragmentary listing I have built up its present length. Most of these terms came from old rails, and especially from boomers, who have written to me as editor of *Railroad Magazine* from all over the United States and Canada.

Even so, this glossary is far from complete. It could be expanded considerably if I were to include for example, the language of the railroad logger. While the logger used many of the mainline railroad words, he coined others to describe the Shay, Heisler, and Climax locomotives which worked the woods. A line has to be drawn somewhere, so I have limited my coverage to the words or expressions that were most widely used by "worthy brothers" of the rail.

Before presenting the glossary, let me cite several "classic" examples which illustrate in exaggerated form how the railroaders talked to one another. The first is an old-timer's account of a trip over a division:

"We was ordered for a train of diamonds, mostly all high hats. The hog came through the hole ten minutes late, and the car-knocker tied him on. Tied in the rubber, and then we tried the wind. We got the high sign from the tent to get out of town, with the advice to 'whale them over the hill.' When we got over the hill, we hit only the high spots until we got to Valley Cottage, where we sawed her off and gave her a drink.

"Then we went down the hill on short time, and jumped a man at Ioan Island who had lost his nerve. Pulled in at Morgans for a high iron dog, followed him out, and went over to Cornwall, where the big smoke filled her up again, while I went in and registered, and asked the op what the muttonhead said. He gave me a message to grab a few more wagons at Newburgh.

"After leavin' Newburgh we canaled along to Kingston, where we grabbed a few more, filled up, and got some more dirt. We had so many that he had to pound her over Saugerties. When we reached Catskill he got about a 35-mile wheel on them to get them over the hump. Then we canaled the rest of the way in."

To the unitiated, the foregoing message sounds like Greek. The translation might read somewhat like this:

"We were ordered for a coal train, consist-ing mostly of big steel gondola cars. After the engine had come through the tunnel ten minutes late, the car inspector coupled her on and we tried the air. We got a go-ahead signal from the caboose to proceed as rapidly as we could.

"When we got over the hill we traveled pretty fast until we reached Valley Cottage. There we cut off the locomotive and got water. Then we went down the hill and passed a man in Iona Island who had lost his nerve. Pulled in at Morgan's sidetrack and let a passenger train go by. Followed him out and dragged over to Cornwall, where the fireman took water, while I went in to register, and I asked the operator what the dispatcher had said. He gave me a message to pick up some cars at Newburgh.

"After we left Newburgh we dragged along to Kingston. There we picked up some more cars, and took on more water and coal. We had so many cars now that the engineer had to work her hard over Saugerties. Reaching Catskill, he got the train going about 35-miles an hour to climb the hill, and then we ran more leisurely the rest of the way in."

The railroad boomer was an itinerant worker who traveled light, skipping at short notice from one division to another, from one railroad to another, from one job to another. His uniform was generally a black "thousand-miler" shirt, so called because he was reputed to wear it on about a thousand miles of rail travel before sending it to the laundry.

The boomer's heyday was roughly the period between the Civil War and shortly after World War I. He was a breed of wanderlust, strikes, liquor, and seasonal rushes such as the movement of melon crops, grain, cattle, and so on, and the ice-locked Great Lakes each winter. Most boomers were actuated by a restless desire to see what lay on the other side of the hill. With his travels, they carried the railroaders' lingo from coast to coast.

The story goes that one time a brakeman on the Milwaukee road was being tried for assault and battery on a switchman. On the witness stand he began: "Your honor, I gave the hoghead a highball to slip the rattlers over the transfer, and the pie-faced snake —"

"Hold on there!" interrupted the judge. "What kind of language do you speak?"

"The same as averyone in West Milwaukee," the brakeman replied.

"Hum," muttered the judge, then he inquired of the court gravely: "Is there an interpreter present who can speak West Milwaukee?"

In another court, a brakeman testified in a suit involving a head-on collision. "The con was flippin' the tissues in the doghouse," he said, "the hind shack was freezin' a hot hub near the hind end, the tallowpot was crackin' diamonds in the tank; the eagle-eye was down greasin' the pig, and I was bendin' the rails when they hit in a cornfield meet."

The English version of this might be: "The conductor was examining his train orders in the cupola, the rear brakeman was cooling an over-heated journal, the fireman was breaking coal, the engineer was oiling the locomotive, and I was throwing a switch when the trains came together head-on."

The porters working the Pullman cars used part of the railroad language and also a few words of their own. In talk among themselves they said "boxcar" when they meant a new type of all-room Pullman. To them a "battleship" was an old-time 16-section sleeper.

In the gaudy lexicon of railroad jargon, the caboose had more names than any other piece of equipment on the high iron, even more than those for engines and engineers. It was called a caboose, crummy, waycar, van, cage, doghouse, drone house, bouncer, bedhouse, buggy, chariot, shelter house, glory wagon, go-cart, hack, hut, monkey wagon, pavilion, palace, parlor, brainbox, zoo, diner, kitchen, perambulator, cabin car, and shanty. There were other names too, which are not printable here.

Suppose you had heard someone say, "The shack was in the angel's seat of the ape wagon, blowing smoke to the Big-O about the time he'd been a baby-lifter on the varnish." Would you have known what he meant? Here is a translation: "The brakeman was in the cupola of the caboose, boasting to the conductor of the time when he had been a brakeman on a passenger train."

The station restaurant or the hash-house or beanery that was often located near the roundhouse, was the source of more old-time colloquialisms than almost anything else connected with railroading. At one time the average railroad man carried a meal ticket which he called "the pie card" and he called the waitress "the beanery queen." Which reminds me of the following tale:

A timid little man sat down at the lunch counter down by the railroad yards and ordered ham and eggs. He looked bewildered when the waitress faced the kitchen and called casually, "A Mogul with two headlights."

A few minutes later the customer asked the waitress: "Beg your pardon, Mam, but can I have those eggs turned over?"

The girl yelled to the cook, "Blanket the headlights!"

Just then an engineer took a seat at the end of the counter and called for some wheatcakes and coffee. He said he was in a hurry.

"Hot running orders," shouted the waitress, truning to a third customer, who had just come in.

"A steak well done," said the last arrival.

"A hotbox and have it smoking," was the information given the cook.

"Scrambled eggs," piped up a gal, and the beanery queen relayed her order as, "A wreck on the main line."

Then a boomer brakeman noisily pushed open the swinging screen door, set down his marker lamps, and mounted one of the stools. "Let's see your switch list," he commanded.

After giving it a quick look he said: "Give me a coupla battleships, a pan of Murphies on the main line, and a string of flats on the siding."

It was the waitress's turn to look mystified.

"Cut the cow car off the Java train," continued the boomer brakeman, "and switch me a coupla life preservers for a Consolidation. It's a long drag to the next feed tank, and you'd better fill the auxiliary to its full capacity."

"Say," cried the biscuit-shooter in dismay, "I've been here only a coupla weeks, and you left me behind at the last stop."

"Excuse me," returned the boomer brakeman. "I thought you were an old head. Give me a couple pork chops, fried potatoes, and a side order of wheatcakes. Also a cup of black coffee and doughnuts. Fill the lunch bucket, too, for it'll be some time before I get to the next restaurant. Put the coffee in the bottom and fill the upper deck with sandwiches and pie."

"I read you Charlie," beamed the girl.

The foregoing is a slightly exaggerated account of scenes that occurred at railroad lunch counters during the days of the boomer. As long as the highly romanticized fiction-stories exist, and as long as books of railroad lore are published, we may expect to read bits of this lost language here and there. Now that railroading has lost its pioneering quality, its steam locomotives, and to some extent even the passenger train, so passes its language. ✧✧✧

Freeman Hubbard, editor of the monthly *Railroad Magazine*, is author of numerous books and articles on rail lore. His best known work, *Railroad Avenue: Great Stories and Legends of American Railroading*, has enthusiastically been adopted as a major contribution to Americana.

ARMSTRONG — Interior of an old fashioned interlocking tower where track switches were thrown by muscle power.

BALLAST SCORCHER — Any engineer making fast time by working his locomotive at full throttle.

AGE—Seniority, length of service

AIR MONKEY—Air-brake repairman

ALLEY—Clear track in railroad *yard*

ANCHOR THEM—Set hand brakes on still cars; the opposite is *release anchors*

ARMSTRONG—Old-style equipment operated by muscular effort, such as hand-brakes, some turntables, engines without automatic stokers, etc.

ARTIST—Man who is particularly adept, usually with prefix such as *brake, pin, speed,* etc.

ASHCAT—Locomotive fireman

BACK TO THE FARM—Laid off on account of slack business. When a man is discharged he is given *six months twice a year*

BAD ORDER—Crippled car or locomotive, often called *cripple*. Must be marked at night by a blue light when men are working around it

BAIL IT IN—Feed the locomotive firebox

BAKEHEAD—Locomotive fireman. Also called *bell ringer, blackie,* and many other names scattered throughout this glossary

BALING-WIRE MECHANIC—A man of little mechanical ability

BALL OF FIRE—Fast run

BALLAST—Turkey or chicken dressing

BALLAST SCORCHER—Speedy engineer

BAND WAGON—Pay car or pay train from which wages were handed out to railroad employees

BANJO—Fireman's shovel; old-style banjo-shaped signal

BAREFOOT—Car or engine without brakes. (Many locomotives built in the 1860's and 1870's were not equipped with brakes except on the tank)

BARN—Locomotive roundhouse, so-called from the building in which streetcars are housed

BAT THE STACK OFF OF HER—Make fast time, work an engine at full stroke

BATTING 'EM OUT—Used generally by switchmen when a *yard* engine is switching a *string* of cars

BATTLESHIP—Large freight engine or interurban car, or a coal car. Also a formidable female, such as the landlady or a henpecked man's wife

BEANERY—Railroad eating house. *Beanery queen* is a waitress

BEANS—*Meet orders;* lunch period

BEAT 'ER ON THE BACK—Make fast time; work an engine at full stroke

BEEHIVE—Railroad *yard* office

BELL RINGER—Locomotive fireman

BEND THE IRON—Change the position of a switch. Also called *bend the rust* or *bend the rail*

BIG BOYS—Special trains for officials

BIG E—Engineer, so called from the large initial on membership buttons of the Brotherhood of Locomotive Engineers

BIG FOUR—The four operating Brotherhoods: Brotherhood of Railroad Trainmen, Order of Railway Conductors, Brotherhood of

Locomotive Firemen and Enginemen, and Brotherhood of Locomotive Engineers

BIG HOLE—Emergency application of air-brake valve, causing a quick stop. *Big-holing her,* the same as *wiping the clock,* is making an emergency stop

BIG HOOK—Wrecking crane

BIG O—Conductor; so named from first initial in Order of Railway Conductors. Sometimes called *big ox* and less complimentary terms

BIG ROCK CANDY MOUNTAINS—Hobo's paradise, as described in song by Harry K. McClintock. (See *Indian Valley Line*)

BINDERS—Hand brakes

BINDLE STIFF or BLANKET STIFF—Hobo who totes a blanket and uses it wherever night finds him. (*Bindle* is a corruption of "bundle")

BIRD CAGE—Brakeman's or switchman's lantern

BLACK DIAMONDS—Company coal. *Diamond cracker* is a locomotive fireman

BLACK HOLE—Tunnel

BLACK ONES—Railway Express refrigerator or boxcars having no interior illumination pressed into mail service during the Christmas rush

BLACK SNAKE—Solid train of loaded coal cars

BLACKBALLED—black-listed, boycotted

BLACKJACKS—Fifty-ton Santa Fe coal cars painted black

BLAZER—Hot journal with packings afire

BLEED—Drain air from. *Bleeder* is valve by which air is bled from auxiliary reservoir of a car

BLIND BAGGAGE—Hobo riding head end of baggage car next to tender, where no door is placed; commonly called *riding the blinds*

BLIZZARD LIGHTS—Originally the lights on either side of the headlight that served in emergency when the oil-burning headlight blew out. Now they indicate the train is nonschedule or extra

BLOOD—Old-time engine built by Manchester Locomotive Works, Mr. Aretas Blood being the builder's name

BLOW 'ER DOWN—Reduce water in a locomotive boiler when carrying too much

BLOW SMOKE—Brag

BLOW UP—Use the blower to increase draft on the fire and thereby raise the steam pressure in the boiler. Also quit a job suddenly

'BO—Hobo. *'Bo chaser* is freight brakeman or railroad policeman

BOARD—Fixed signal regulating railroad traffic, usually referred to as *slow board, order board, clear board* (for clear tracks) or *red board* (stop). Do not confuse this with *extra board* or *spare board,* colloquially known as *slow board* or *starvation list,* usually containing names of qualified train or enginemen not in regular active service who are called to work in emergencies. These names are listed in order of seniority, the man hired most recently being the last one called to service

BOBTAIL—Switch engine

BOILER ASCENSION—Boiler explosion

BOILER HEADER—Man riding in engine cab

BIRD CAGE — The oil lantern carried by trainmen.

BLACK HOLE — A railroad tunnel or series of tunnels.

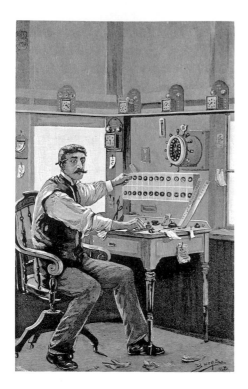

BRASS POUNDER — A railroad operator who dispatched and received train orders by telegraph. Often referred to as a lightning slinger".

BUCKLE THE RUBBER — An expression used by switchmen when connecting the rubber air hoses after coupling the cars.

BOILER WASH—A high-water engineer

BOOK OF RULES—Examination based on facts in rulebook

BOOKKEEPER—Trainman who makes out reports; flagman

BOOTLEGGER—Train that runs over more than one railroad

BOOMER—Drifter who went from one railroad job to another, staying but a short time on each job or each road. This term dates back to pioneer days when men followed boom camps. The opposite is *home guard*. Boomers should not be confused with tramps, although they occasionally became tramps. *Boomers* were railroad workers often in big demand because of their wide experience, sometimes blackballed because their tenure of stay was uncertain. Their common practice was to follow the "rushes"—that is, to apply for seasonal jobs when and where they were most needed, when the movement of strawberry crops, watermelons, grain, etc., was making the railroads temporarily short-handed. There are virtually no *boomers* in North America today. When men are needed for seasonal jobs they are called from the *extra board*

BOUNCER—Caboose

BOWLING ALLEY—Hand-fired coal-burning locomotive. (A fireman throwing in the lumps of coal goes through motions that resemble bowling)

BOXCAR TOURIST—Hobo

BRAIN PLATE—Trainman's cap or hat badge

BRAINS or THE BRAINS—Conductor; sometimes called *brainless wonder*, a term also applied to any train or engineman or official who does things his fellows consider queer

BRAKE CLUB—Three-foot hickory stick used by freight trainmen to tighten hand brakes. Sometimes called *sap* or *staff of ignorance*

BRASS—A babbitt-lined blank of bronze that forms the bearing upon which the car rests. To *brass* a car is to replace one of those bearings

BRASS BUTTONS—Passenger conductor on railroad or streetcar line

BRASS COLLAR or BRASS HAT—Railroad official. Term may have originated from gold-braided collar of conductor's uniform and brass plate on his cap

BRASS POUNDER—Telegraph operator

BREEZE—Service air

BRIDGE HOG—Bridge and building carpenter of the old school antedating steel and concrete

BROKEN KNUCKLES—Railroad sleeping quarters

BROWNIES—Demerits. This system is traced back to George R. Brown, general superintendent of the Fall Brook Railway (now part of the New York Central) in 1885. He thought the then current practice of suspending men for breaking rules was unfair to their families and substituted a system of demerit marks. Too many demerits in a given period resulted in dismissal. The Brown system, with many variations, has since been widely adopted by the railroad industry. A superintendent's private car is called *brownie box* or *brownie wagon*

BUCK THE BOARD—Working the *extra board*. (See *board*)

BUCKLE THE RUBBERS—Connect air, steam, or signal hose

BUG—Telegraph instrument or trainman's or switchman's light, which is also called *bug torch*. *Bug* may also be a three-wheeled electric truck that carries mail and baggage around terminals

BUG LINE—Telephone connection between engine house and *yard* or telegraph office

BUG SLINGER—Switchman or brakeman

BUGGY—Caboose; rarely applied to other cars

BULL—Railroad policeman. Also called *flatfoot* or *gumshoe*, but the distinctive railroad terms are *cinder dick* and *'bo chaser*

BULL PEN—Crew room

BULLGINE—Steam locomotive

BULLNOSE—Front drawbar of a locomotive

BUMP—Obtain another man's position by exercising seniority. When a crew is deprived of its assignment, as when a train is removed from the timetable, its members select the jobs they wish from those held by others with less *whiskers*

BUMPER—Post at end of spur track, placed there to stop rolling stock from running onto the ground

BUNCH OF THIEVES—Wrecking crew

BUST UP A CUT—To separate the cars in a train, removing some that have reached their destination, assigning others to through trains, etc.

BUTTERFLY—Note thrown (or handed) from train by an official to a section foreman or other employee, so called because it may flutter along the track, although it is usually weighted down when thrown from a car

BUZZARDS' ROOST—Yard office

CABOOSE BOUNCE, CABOOSE HOP—Early term for a train composed only of an engine and caboose

CAGE—Caboose

CALLER—One whose duty is to summon train or engine crews or announce trains

CALLIOPE—Steam locomotive

CAMEL or CAMELBACK—Engine with control cab built over middle of boiler, suggesting camel's hump. Also called *Mother Hubbard* type

CAN—Tank car

CANNED—Taken out of service

CAPTAIN—Conductor; often called *skipper*. This title dates from Civil War days when some railroads were run by the Army and the conductor was in many cases a captain

CAR-CATCHER—Rear brakeman

CAR KNOCKER—Car inspector or car repairer—from the early custom of tapping the wheels to detect flaws. Also called *car whacker;* and *car toad* (because he squats while inspecting), *car tink,* and *car tonk*

CAR-SEAL HAWK—Railroad policeman

CARD—Credentials showing Brotherhood or Union membership

CARHOUSE CAR—Covered cement car

CARRY A WHITE FEATHER—Show a plume of steam over the safety valves of the engine

BUGGY — One of the many terms for the familiar caboose.

CATWALK — The wooden walkway on top of the freight cars. This walk was used by brakemen moving from one car to another while the train was in motion. In the days before automatic air brakes, the engineer would signal the brakemen by a code on the whistle. The brakemen would rush to tie down the hand brakes to slow the speed of the train.

CARRYING GREEN—Train whose engine displays green flags by day or green lights by night to indicate that a second section is following closely. *Carrying white* in the same manner signifies an extra train

CARRYING THE BANNER—Flagging. Also wearing ostentatious Brotherhood emblems, frequently done by *'bos* in working the main stem for a handout

CARRYING THE MAIL—Bringing train orders

CASEY JONES—Any locomotive engineer, especially a fast one. Name derived from John Luther (Casey) Jones

CATWALK—Plank walk on top of boxcars; sometimes called the *deck* from which comes the word *deckorate*

CHAIN GANG—Crew assigned to pool service, working first in, first out

CHAMBERMAID—Machinist in roundhouse

CHARIOT—Caboose, or general manager's car

CHASING THE RED—Flagman going back with red flag or light to protect his train

CHECKER—A company spy, particularly one checking up on loss of materials or of the receipts of an agent or conductor

CHERRY PICKER—Switchman, so called because of red lights on switch stands. Also any railroad man who is always figuring on the best jobs and sidestepping undesirable ones (based on the old allusion, "Life is a bowl of cherries")

CHEW CINDERS—Engines do this when reversed while running and while working quite a bit of steam

CHIPPIES—Narrow-gauge cars

CINDER CRUNCHER—Switchman or flagman. *Cinder skipper* is yard clerk

CINDER DICK—Railroad policeman or detective

CINDER SNAPPER—Passenger who rides open platforms on observation car

CIRCUS—Railroad

CLAW—Clinker hook used by fireman

CLEARANCE CARD—Authority to use main line

CLOCK—Steam gauge. (See *wiping the clock;* don't confuse with *Dutch clock*). Also fare register

CLOWN—Switchman or yard brakeman. *Clown wagon* is caboose

CLUB—Same as *brake club. Club winder* is switchman or brakeman. A brakeman's club was usually his only weapon of defense against hoboes

COAL HEAVER—Fireman, sometimes called stoker

COCK-LOFT—Cupola of a caboose. Also called *crow's nest*

COFFEE—Respite period enjoyed by baggagemen while awaiting arrival of the next train. Also called *spot*

COFFEEPOT—Little, old, steam locomotive

COLLAR AND ELBOW JOINT—Boardinghouse. (There isn't too much room at dinner table)

COLOR-BLIND—Employee who can't distinguish between his own money and the company's

COMPANY BIBLE—Book of rules

COMPANY JEWELRY—Trainman's hat, badge, and switch keys

COMPANY NOTCH or WALL STREET NOTCH—Forward corner of the reverse gear quadrant. It is called the *company notch* because an engine exerts full pulling power when worked with a full stroke

CONDUCER—Conductor

CONSIST—Contents or equipment of a train. Report form sent ahead so yardmaster can make plans for switching the train. The report is usually dropped off to an operator; this is *dropping the consist*

COOL A SPINDLE—Cool a hotbox by replacing the brass or putting water on the bearing

COON IT—Crawl

CORNERED—When a car, not in the clear on a siding, is struck by a train or engine

CORNFIELD MEET—Head-on collision or one that is narrowly averted

COULDN'T PULL A SETTING HEN OFF HER NEST—Derogatory description of old-fashioned locomotive

COUNTING THE TIES—Reducing speed

COW CAGE—Stock car. Also called *cow crate*

COWCATCHER—Pilot. The old term was discarded by railroad officials, probably because it was a butt for jokesters. You've often heard about the passenger on a slow local train complaining to the conductor, "I don't understand why you have the *cowcatcher* on the front of the engine. This train can never overtake a cow. But if you'd attach it to the rear of the train it might at least discourage cows from climbing into the last car and annoying the passengers"

CRADLE—Gondola or other open-top car

CRIB—Caboose

CRIPPLE—See *bad order*

CROAKER—Company doctor

CROWNING HIM—Coupling a caboose on a freight train when it is made up

CRUMB BOSS—Man in charge of camp cars

CRUMMY—Caboose. Also called *crum box*, *crib*, and many other names. Innumerable poems have been written about "the little red caboose behind the train"

CUPOLA—Observation tower on caboose

CUSHIONS—Passenger cars. *Cushion rider* may be either a passenger or member of passenger-train crew. (See *varnished cars*)

CUT—Several cars attached to an engine or coupled together by themselves. Also that part of the right-of-way which is excavated out of a hill or mountain instead of running up over it or being tunneled through it

CUT THE BOARD—Lay off the most recently hired men on the extra list. (See *board*)

DANCING ON THE CARPET—Called to an official's office for investigation or discipline

DEAD IRON and LIVE IRON—The two sets of tracks on a scale

DEAD MAN'S HOLE—Method of righting an overturned engine or car. A six-foot hole is dug about forty feet from the engine or car, long enough to hold a large solid-oak plank. A trench is then dug

CORNFIELD MEET — A head-on collision between two locomotives or cars on the same track.

DANCING ON THE CARPET — Crews called it "Dancing on the Carpet" when they were called into an official's office for an investigation or violation of the Book of Rules.

up to the engine and heavy ropes laid in it, with a four-sheave block, or pulley, at the lower end of the engine and a three-sheave block at the top of the boiler. Chains are fastened to the underside of the engine and hooked to the three-sheave block. The free end of the rope is then hooked to the drawbar of a road engine. The hole is filled—packed hard to hold the "dead man" down against the coming pull. When the engine moves up the track she pulls ropes over the top of the boiler of the overturned locomotive on the chains that are fastened to the lower part, rolling the engine over sidewise and onto her wheels again

DEAD MAN'S THROTTLE—Throttle that requires pressure of operator's hand or foot to prevent power shut-off and application of brakes. An engine so equipped would stop instantly if the operator fell dead. Also called *dead man's button*

DEADHEAD—Employee riding on a pass; any nonpaying passenger. Also fireman's derisive term for head brakeman who rides engine cab. Also a locomotive being hauled "dead" on a train

DECK—Front part of engine cab. Also *catwalk* on roofs of boxcars

DECKORATE—Get out on top of freight cars to set hand brakes or receive or transmit signals. Derived from *deck*

DEHORNED—Demoted or discharged

DETAINER or DELAYER—Train dispatcher

DIAMOND—Railroad crossover. *Black diamonds* is coal

DIAMOND CRACKER or DIAMOND PUSHER—Locomotive fireman

DIE GAME—Stall on a hill

DING-DONG—Gas or gas-electric coach, usually used on small roads or branch lines not important enough to support regular trains; name derived from sound of its bell. Sometimes called *doodlebug*

DINGER—Conductor (man who rings the bell)

DINKY—Switch engine without tender, used around back shop and roundhouse, or any small locomotive. Also a four-wheel trolleycar

DIPLOMA—Clearance or service letter; fake service letter

DIRTY CAR—Storage car containing a varied assortment of mail and parcels that demand extra work in separating

DISHWASHERS—Engine wipers at roundhouse

DITCH—That part of the right-of-way that is lower than the roadbed. A derailed train is "in the ditch"

DOGCATCHERS—Crew sent out to relieve another that has been *outlawed*—that is, overtaken on the road by the sixteen-hour law, which is variously known as *dog law*, *hog law*, and *pure-food law*

DOGHOUSE—Caboose or its cupola

DONEGAN—Old car, with wheels removed, used as residence or office. Originated about 1900, when a Jersey Central carpenter and two foremen, all named Donegan, occupied three shacks in the same vicinity. People were directed to the Donegans so often that the shacks themselves came to be known by that name. The name stuck, even after the men had passed on and the shacks had been replaced by converted old cars

DONKEY—Derisive term for section man; small auxiliary engine

DINKY—A four-wheeled switch engine without tender. It was used around the company shops or roundhouse to move cars and locomotives whose fire was dead.

DOODLEBUG—Rail motorcar used by section men, linemen, etc. Also called *ding dong*

DOPE—Order, official instructions, explanation. Also a composition for cooling hot journals

DOPE IT—Use compound in the water to keep it from boiling when working an engine hard

DOPE MONKEY—Car inspector

DOUBLE—In going up a hill, to cut the train in half and take each section up separately

DOUBLE-HEADER—Train hauled by two engines

DOUSE THE GLIM—Extinguish a lantern, especially by a sudden upward movement

DRAG—Heavy train of "dead" freight; any slow freight train, as contrasted with *manifest* or *hotshot*

DRAWBAR FLAGGING—Flagman leaning against the drawbar on the caboose, or standing near the caboose, to protect the rear end of his train, instead of going back "a sufficient distance" as rules require. Such a man is taking a chance, due maybe to laziness, exhaustion, severe cold, fear of the train leaving without him, etc.

DRIFTING THROTTLE—Running with steam throttle cracked open to keep air and dust from being sucked into steam cylinders

DRILL CREW—*Yard* crew. (See *yard*)

DRINK—Water for locomotive

DRONE CAGE—Private car

DROP—Switching movement in which cars are cut off from an engine and allowed to coast to their places. (See *hump*)

DROP A LITTLE RUN-FAST—Oil the engine

DROP 'ER DOWN—Pull reverse lever forward. *Drop 'er in the corner* means to make fast time, figuratively dropping the *Johnson bar* in one corner of the cab

DROPPER—Switchman riding a car on a hump

DROWNING IT OUT—Cooling an overheated journal

DRUMMER—Yard conductor

DRUNKARD—Late Saturday-night passenger train

DUCATS—Passenger conductor's hat checks

DUDE—Passenger conductor

DUDE WRANGLER—Passenger brakeman

DUMMY—Employees' train. *Dummy locomotive* is a switcher type having the boiler and running gear entirely housed, used occasionally for service in public streets

DUST-RAISER—Fireman (shoveling coal into firebox)

DUSTING HER OUT—Putting sand through the firedoor of an oil burner while working the engine hard; this cuts out the soot in the flues and makes the locomotive steam. Also known as *giving the old girl a dose of salts*

DUTCH CLOCK—Speed recorder

DUTCH DROP—Rarely used method of bringing a car onto the main line from a spur. The engine heads into the spur, couples head-on to the car, and backs out. When the car is moving fast enough the engine is cut off, speeds up to get back on the main line before the car,

DRINK—Taking water into the tender of a locomotive from a trackside spout or tank.

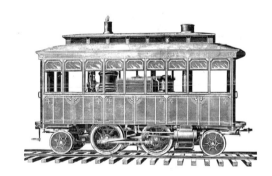

DUMMY—A locomotive whose boiler and running gear had been covered. Locomotives of this type were often used in public streets so as not to excite the horses. The above engine was built for the New York Metropolitan Railroad (1877) by the Grant Locomotive Works.

then moves forward ahead of the junction between the main line and the spur so the car rolls out behind the engine

DYNAMITER—Car on which defective mechanism sends the brakes into full emergency when only a service application is made by the engineer. Also, a quick-action triple valve

EAGLE-EYE—Locomotive engineer

EASY SIGN—Signal indicating the train is to move slowly

END MAN—Rear brakeman on freight train

ELECTRIC OWL—Night operator

ELEPHANT CAR—Special car coupled behind locomotive to accommodate head brakeman

EXTRA BOARD—See *board*

EYE—Trackside signal

FAMILY DISTURBER—Pay car or pay train

FAN—Blower on a locomotive boiler

FIELD—Classification *yard*

FIELDER or FIELD MAN—*Yard* brakeman

FIGUREHEAD—Timekeeper

FIREBOY—Locomotive fireman

FIRST READER—Conductor's train book

FISH WAGON—Gas-electric car or other motorcar equipped with an air horn (which sounds like a fishmonger's horn)

FISHTAIL—Semaphore blade, so called from its peculiar shape

FIST—Telegraph operator's handwriting. This script, in the days before telephones, typewriters, and teletypes, was characterized by its swiftness, its bold flowing curves which connected one word with another, and its legibility. *Ops* were proud of their penmanship

FIXED MAN—Switchman in a *hump* yard assigned to one certain post from which he rides cars being humped

FIXED SIGNAL—Derisive term for a student brakeman standing on a boxcar with his lamp out and a cinder in his eye

FLAG—Assumed name. Many a *boomer* worked *under a flag* when his own name was black-listed

FLAT—Flatcar. Also called *car with the top blowed off*

FLAT WHEEL—Car wheel that has flat spots on the tread. Also applied to an employee who limps

FLIMSY—Train order. (Standard practice is to issue these on tissue paper to facilitate the making of carbon copies)

FLIP—To board a moving train. The word accurately suggests the motion used

FLOATER—Same as *boomer*

FLY LIGHT—Miss a meal. *Boomers* often did that; hoboes still do

FLYING SWITCH—Switching technique in which the engine pulls away from a car or cars she has started rolling, permitting them to be switched onto a track other than that taken by the engine. The switch is thrown instantly after the engine has passed it and just before the cars reach it. This procedure, common in bygone days, is now frowned upon by officials

FOG—Steam

EAGLE EYE — A locomotive engineer with the ability to see or observe the track and signals with exceptional keenness.

FOOTBOARD—The step on the rear and front ends of switch or freight engines. Many casualties were caused in the "good old days" by switchmen missing these steps on dark slippery nights

FOOTBOARD YARDMASTER—Conductor who acts as yardmaster in a small *yard*

FOREIGN CAR—Car running over any railroad other than the one that owns it

FOUNTAIN—That part of a locomotive where steam issues from the boiler and flows into pipes for lubrication, injection, etc.

FREEZE A HOB or A BLAZER—Cool a heated journal

FREEZER—Refrigerator car. Also *reefer* or *riff*

FROG—Implement for rerailing cars or engines. Also an X-shaped plate where two tracks cross

FUSEE—Red flare used for flagging purposes. Its sharp point is driven into the right-of-way and no following train may pass as long as it is burning, although on some roads it is permissible to stop, extinguish the *fusee*, and proceed with caution in automatic block-signal limits

GALLOPER—Locomotive, the *iron horse*

GALLOPING GOOSE—A shaky section car

GALVANIZER—Car inspector

GANDY DANCER—Track laborer. Name may have originated from the gander-like tremulations of a man tamping ties, or from the old Gandy Manufacturing Company of Chicago, which made tamping bars, claw bars, picks, and shovels

GANGWAY—Space between the rear cab post of a locomotive and her tender

GARDEN—See *yard*

GAS HOUSE—Yard office

GATE—Switch

GAY CAT—Tramp held in contempt by fellow vagrants because he is willing to work if a job comes along

GENERAL—Yardmaster, abbreviated Y.M.

GET THE ROCKING CHAIR—Retire on a pension

GET YOUR HEAD CUT IN—Boomer slang for "wise up"

GIRL or OLD GIRL—Affectionate term for steam engine. The locomotive, like the sailing ship, is often called "she" instead of "it"

GIVE HER THE GRIT—Use sand

GLASS CARS—Passenger cars

GLIM—Switchman's or trainman's lantern

GLIMMER—Locomotive headlight

GLORY—String of empty cars. Also death, especially by accident

GLORY HUNTER—Reckless, fast-running engineer

GLORY ROAD—Sentimental term for railroad

GOAT—*Yard* engine. (See *yard*)

GOAT FEEDER—Yard fireman

GO HIGH—Same as *deckorate*

G.M.—General manager. G.Y.M. is general yardmaster

GODS OF IRON—Huge, powerful locomotives

GON—Gondola, or steel-sided, flat-bottom coal car

GO-TO-HELL SIGNAL — A signal given by violent motion of the hand or by waving a lantern. Often meant a wreck or derailment ahead on the track.

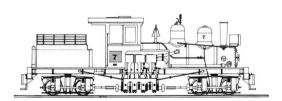

GRIND — A Shay geared locomotive used in logging regions where the grade is steep and the track rough.

GONE FISHING—Laid off

GOO-GOO EYE—Locomotive with two firedoors

GOOSE—To make an emergency stop

GOOSE HER—Reverse a locomotive that is under headway

GO-TO-HELL SIGNAL—Signal given with violent motion of hand or lantern

GRAB IRON—Steel bar attached to cars and engines as a hand hold

GRABBER—Conductor of a passenger train. (He grabs tickets)

GRAMOPHONE—Obsolete term for telephone

GRASS WAGON—Tourist car. (Tourists like scenery)

GRASSHOPPER—Old type of locomotive with vertical boiler and cylinders

GRAVE-DIGGER—Section man

GRAVEYARD—Siding occupied by obsolete and disused engines and cars; scrap pile

GRAVEYARD WATCH—12.01 A.M. to 8 A.M., or any midnight shift, so called because that shift includes the quietest hours of the day

GRAZING TICKET—Meal book

GREASE MONKEY—Car oiler

GREASE THE PIG—Oil the engine. (See *hog*)

GREASY SPOON—Railroad eating house. Bill of fare is colloquially known as *switch list*, fork is *hook*, butter is *grease pot*, hotcakes are *blind gaskets*, and beans are *torpedoes*

GREENBACKS—*Frogs* for rerailing engines or cars

GREENBALL FREIGHT—Fruit or vegetables

GREEN EYE—Clear signal. (At the time Cy Warman wrote his celebrated poem, "I Hope the Lights Are White," the clear signal was white and green meant caution. This was changed years ago because of the fact that when a red or green signal lens broke or fell out it exposed a white, thus giving a *clear board* to engineers even though the signal itself was set to stop or go slow)

GREETINGS FROM THE DS—Train orders from the dispatcher

GRIEVER—Spokesman on grievance committee; Brotherhood or Union representative at an official investigation

GRIND—Shay-geared engine

GROUNDHOG—Brakeman, yardmaster, or switch engine

GRUNT—Locomotive engineer. *Traveling grunt* is road foreman of engines (hogs). *Grunt* may also be a lineman's ground helper; *grunting* is working as a lineman's helper

GUN—Torpedo, part of trainman's equipment; it is placed on the track as a signal to the engineer. Also the injector on the locomotive that forces water from tank to boiler. *To gun* means to control air-brake system from rear of train

GUNBOAT—Large steel car

GUT—Air hose. *Guts* is drawbar

HACK—Caboose

HALF—Period of two weeks

HAM—Poor telegrapher or student

HAND BOMBER or HAND GRENADE—Engine without automatic stoker, which is hand-fired

HAND-ON—Train order or company mail caught with the hoop or without stopping

HANGING UP THE CLOCK—*Boomer* term that meant hocking your railroad watch

HARNESS—Passenger trainman's uniform

HASH HOUSE—Railroad restaurant or lunch stand

HAT—Ineffectual railroad man. (All he uses his head for is a hat rack)

HAY—Sleep on the job; any kind of sleep. Caboose was sometimes called *hay wagon*

HAY BURNER—Hand oil lantern, inspection torch. Also a horse used in railroad or streetcar service

HEAD-END REVENUE—Money which railroads receive for hauling mail, express, baggage, newspapers, and milk in cans, usually transported in cars nearest the locomotive, these commodities or shipments being known as *head-end traffic*

HEAD IN—Take a sidetrack when meeting an opposing train

HEAD MAN—Front brakeman on a freight train who rides the engine cab. Also called *head pin*

HEARSE—Caboose

HEEL—Cars on end of tracks with brakes applied

HERDER—Man who couples engines and takes them off upon arrival and departure of trains

HIGHBALL—Signal made by waving hand or lamp in a high, wide semicircle, meaning "Come ahead" or "Leave town" or "Pick up full speed." Verb *highball* or phrase *'ball the jack* means to make a fast run. Word *highball* originated from old-time ball signal on post, raised aloft by pulley when track was clear. A very few of these are still in service, in New England and elsewhere

HIGHBALL ARTIST—A locomotive engineer known for fast running

HIGH-DADDY—*Flying switch*

HIGH IRON—Main line or high-speed track (which is laid with heavier rail than that used on unimportant branches or spurs)

HIGHLINER—Main-line fast passenger train

HIGH-WHEELER—Passenger engine or fast passenger train. Also *highball artist*

HIKER—A lineman who "hikes sticks" instead of prosaically climbing poles

HIT 'ER—Work an engine harder. (Probably a variation of "hit the ball," which means "Get busy—no more fooling!")

HIT THE GRIT or GRAVEL—Fall off a car or locomotive or get kicked off

HOBO—Tramp. Term is said to have originated on Burlington Route as a corruption of "Hello, boy!" which construction workers used in greeting one another

HOG—Any large locomotive, usually freight. An engineer may be called a *hogger, hoghead, hogmaster, hoggineer, hog jockey, hog eye, grunt, pig-mauler,* etc. Some few engineers object to such designations as disrespectful, which they rarely are. For meaning of *hog law* see *dogcatchers. Hoghead* is said to have originated on the Denver & Rio Grande in 1887, being used to label a brakeman's caricature of an engineer

HIGHBALL — A signal made by waving the hand in a wide semicircle. This gesture told the engineer to "Come Ahead" or "Leave Town".

HOLDING HER AGAINST THE BRASS—Running electric car at full speed

HOLE—Passing track where one train pulls in to meet another

HOME GUARD—Employee who stays with one railroad, as contrasted with *boomer*. A *homesteader* is a *boomer* who gets married and settles down

HOOK—Wrecking crane or auxiliary

HOOK 'ER UP AND PULL HER TAIL—To set the reverse lever up on the quadrant and pull the throttle well out for high speed

HOPPER—Steel-sided car with a bottom that opens to allow unloading of coal, gravel, etc.

HOPTOAD—Derail

HORSE 'ER OVER—Reverse the engine. This is done by compressed air on modern locomotives, but in early days, manually operated reversing equipment required considerable jockeying to reverse an engine while in motion

HOSE COUPLER—Brakeman who handles trains by himself with the road engine around a big passenger terminal

HOSTLER—Any employee (usually a fireman) who services engines, especially at division points and terminals. Also called *ashpit engineer*

HOT—Having plenty of steam pressure (applied to locomotives)

HOT-FOOTER—Engineer or conductor in switching service who is always in a hurry

HOT JEWEL—Same as *hotbox*

HOT-WATER BOTTLE—Elesco feed water heater

HOT WORKER—Boilermaker who repairs leaks in the firebox or flue sheet while there is pressure in the boiler

HOTBOX—Overheated journal or bearing. Also called *hub*. This was a frequent cause of delay in the old days but is virtually nonexistent on trains that are completely equipped with ball-bearings. Trainmen are sometimes called *hotbox detectors*

HOTSHOT—Fast train; frequently a freight made up of merchandise and perishables. Often called a *manifest* or *redball* run

HOW MANY EMS HAVE YOU GOT?—How many thousand pounds of tonnage is your engine pulling? (M stands for 1,000)

HUMP—Artificial knoll at end of classification yard over which cars are pushed so that they can roll on their own momentum to separate tracks. (See *drop*.) Also the summit of a hill division or the top of a prominent grade. *Boomers* generally referred to the Continental Divide as the *Hump*

HUMPBACK JOB—Local freight run. (Conductor spends much time in caboose bending over his wheel reports)

HUT—Brakeman's shelter just back of the coal bunkers on the tender tank of engines operating through Moffat Tunnel. May also refer to caboose, locomotive cab, switchman's shanty, or crossing watchman's shelter

IDLER—An unloaded flatcar placed before or after a car from which oversize machinery, pipe, or other material projects

IN—A trainman who is at the home terminal and off duty is *in*

IN THE CLEAR—A train is *in the clear* when it has passed over a switch and frog so far that another train can pass without damage

HOTBOX — An overheated wheel journal often delayed trains in the days before roller bearings. A "hotbox" provided entertainment for curious passengers.

IN THE COLOR—Train standing in the signal block waiting for a *clear board*

IN THE DITCH—Wrecked or derailed

IN THE HOLE—On a siding. (See *hole*.) Also in the lower berth of a Pullman, as contrasted with *on the top*, in the upper berth

INDIAN VALLEY LINE—An imaginary railroad "at the end of the rainbow," on which you could always find a good job and ideal working conditions. (Does not refer to the former twenty-one-mile railroad of that name between Paxton and Engels, Calif.) *Boomers* resigning or being fired would say they were going to the *Indian Valley*. The term is sometimes used to mean death or the railroader's Heaven. (See *Big Rock Candy Mountains*)

INDICATORS—Illuminated signs on the engine and caboose that display the number of the train

IRON or RAIL—Track. *Single iron* means single track

IRON HORSE—Academic slang for locomotive

IRON SKULL—Boilermaker. (Jim Jeffries, one-time champion prize fighter, worked as an *iron skull* for years)

IN THE DITCH — A locomotive or piece of equipment which had left the rails and rested in a ditch, stream or down an embankment.

JACK—Locomotive. (A term often confused with the lifting device, hence seldom used)

JACKPOT—Miscellaneous assortment of mail and parcels piled in the aisle of a baggage car and requiring removal before the mail in the stalls can be "worked"

JAILHOUSE SPUDS—Waffled potatoes

JAM BUSTER—Assistant yardmaster

JAM NUTS—Doughnuts

JANNEY—To couple; derived from the Janney automatic coupler

JAWBONE SHACK—Switch shanty

JAY ROD—Clinker hook

JERK A DRINK—Take water from track pan without stopping train. From this came the word *jerkwater*, which usually means a locality serving only to supply water to the engines of passing trains; a place other than a regular stop, hence of minor importance as *jerkwater* town, *jerkwater* college, etc.

JERK-BY—See *flying switch*

JERK SOUP—Same as *jerk a drink*

JERRY—Section worker; sometimes applied to other laborers

JEWEL—Journal brass

JIGGER—Full tonnage of "dead" freight

JIMMIES—Four-wheel coal or ore cars

JITNEY—Four-wheel electric truck that carries baggage around inside a terminal. Also unregulated private automobile that carried passengers on public highways for 5-cent fare in direct competition with trolley cars

JOHNSON BAR—Reverse lever on a locomotive. (See *drop 'er down*)

JOIN THE BIRDS—Jump from moving engine or car, usually when a wreck is imminent

JOINT—A length of rail, generally 33 or 39 feet. *Riding to a joint* is bringing cars together so that they couple

JOKER—Independent or locomotive brake

JOIN THE BIRDS—The jump from a moving locomotive or car when a wreck or derailment was imminent.

LINK AND PIN — The old type of coupler used in the early days of railroading. Consisted of a metal loop which coupled two cars together, and called the link. A pin held the link in position.

LIFT TRANSPORTATION — The collecting of tickets by the passenger conductor.

JUGGLER—Member of way-freight crew who loads and unloads *LCL* freight at station stops

JUGGLING THE CIRCLE—Missing a train-order hoop

JUICE—Electricity. *Juice fan* is one who makes a hobby out of electric railways (*juice lines*)

JUNK PILE—Old worn-out locomotive that is still in service.

KANGAROO COURT—An official hearing or investigation, so named because it may be held wherever most convenient, anywhere along the road, jumping around like a kangaroo, to act on main-line mix-ups or other urgent problems

KEELEY—Water can for hot journals or bearings. Nickname derived from "Keeley cure" for liquor habit

KETTLE—Any small locomotive, especially an old, leaky one. Also called *teakettle* and *coffeepot*

KEY—Telegraph instrument

KICK—See *drop*

KICKER—Triple valve in defective order, which throws air brakes into emergency when only a service application is intended, or sometimes by a bump of the train

KING—Freight conductor or yardmaster. *King snipe* is foreman of track gang. *King pin* is conductor

KITCHEN—Caboose; engine cab. Firebox is *kitchen stove*

KNOCKOUT—Same as *bump*

KNOWLEDGE BOX—Yardmaster's office; president of the road

LADDER—Main track of *yard* from which individual tracks lead off. Also called a *lead*. (See *yard*)

LAPLANDER—Passenger jostled into someone else's lap in crowded car

LAST CALL, LAST TERMINAL, etc.—Death

LAY-BY—Passing track, sidetrack. *Layed out* is delayed

LAY OVER—Time spent waiting for connection with other train

LCL—Less than carload lots of freight

LETTERS—Service letters given to men who resign or are discharged. Applicants for railroad jobs are usually asked to present *letters* proving previous employment. In the old days, when these were too unfavorable, many boomers used faked *letters* or would work *under a flag* on somebody else's certificates

LEVER JERKER—Interlocker lever man

LIBRARY—Cupola of caboose. Trainman occupying it was sometimes known as a *librarian*

LIFT TRANSPORTATION—Collect tickets

LIGHT ENGINE—An engine moving outside the *yard* without cars attached

LIGHTNING SLINGER—Telegraph operator

LINER—Passenger train

LINK AND PIN—Old-time type of coupler; used to denote old-fashioned methods of railroading

LIZARD SCORCHER—Dining-car chef

LOADS—Loaded freight cars

LOCAL LOAD—A truckload of mail in sacks and parcels sent from the storage car direct to a car on a local train, containing mail for towns along the route of the train

LOUSE CAGE—Caboose

LUNAR WHITE—The color of white used on all switches except on main line

LUNCH HOOKS—Your two hands

LUNG—Drawbar or air hose

LUNG DOCTOR—Locomotive engineer who pulls out drawbars. Also *lung specialist*

MADHOUSE—Engine foreman; scene of unusual activity or confusion

MAIN IRON—Main track. Also called *main stem*

MAIN PIN—An official

MAKE A JOINT—Couple cars

MANIFEST—Same as *hotshot*

MARKERS—Signals on rear of train, flags by day and lamps by night

MASTER MANIAC—Master mechanic, often abbreviated M.M. Oil is called *master mechanic's blood*

MASTER MIND—An official

MATCHING DIALS—Comparing time

MAUL—Work an engine with full stroke and full throttle

MEAT RUN—Fast run of perishable freight, *hotshot*

MEET ORDER—Train order specifying a definite location where two or more trains will meet on a single track, one on a siding, the others on the *high iron*

MERRY GO-ROUND—Turntable

MIDDLE MAN, MIDDLE SWING—Second brakeman on freight train

MIKE—Mikado-type engine (2-8-2), so named because first of this type were built for Imperial Railways of Japan. (Because of the war with Japan, some railroads rechristened this type *MacArthur*)

MILEAGE HOG—Engineer or conductor, paid on mileage basis, who uses his seniority to the limit in getting good runs, which younger men resent

MILK TRUCK—Large hand truck with high cast-iron wheels used to transfer milk cans around in a terminal

MILL—Steam locomotive, or typewriter

MIXED LOAD—Truckload of mail sacks and parcels for many destinations sent from *storage car* to the *yard* (an outside platform) for further separation before forwarding

MONKEY—When a crew has been on duty sixteen hours and is caught out on the road, *the monkey gets them* and they are required by ICC rules to *tie up* until a new crew comes. (See *dogcatchers*)

MONKEY MONEY—The pass of a passenger who is riding free

MONKEY MOTION—Walschaert or Baker valve gear on locomotive. *Monkey house* is caboose. *Monkey suit* is passenger trainman's uniform or any other smart-looking uniform. *Monkey tail* is back-up hose

MOONLIGHT MECHANIC—Night roundhouse foreman

MOPPING OFF—Refers to escaping steam

MOTHER HUBBARD—See *Camelback*

MARKERS—Signals on the rear of a train, flags by day and lamps by night.

MERRY-GO-ROUND — A revolving horizontal plane used for turning locomotives and cars, more often called a turntable. In the early days the turntable was hand powered and located in the center of the roundhouse.

MOTOR—Electric locomotive

MOUNTAIN PAY—Overtime

MOVING DIRT—Fireman shoveling coal into firebox

MOVING SPIRIT—Train dispatcher, more often called DS

MTYS—Empty cars

MUCKERS—Excavators in construction work

MUD CHICKENS—Surveyor. *Mudhop* is yard clerk, *mudshop* his office

MUD SUCKER—A nonlifting injector

MUDHEN—A saturated locomotive, one that is not superheated

MULE SKINNER—Driver of mule cart

MUSIC MASTER—Paymaster

MUTT AND JEFF PUMP—Denver & Rio Grande locomotive with big air pump on right and small one on left

MUZZLE LOADER—Hand-fired locomotive

NEWS BUTCHER—Peddler who sells magazines, candy, fruit, etc., in trains. Usually employed nowadays by Union News Co. Thomas A. Edison, the inventor, was a *news butcher* in his youth and became deaf when a conductor boxed his ears for accidentally starting a fire while experimenting in a baggage car near Smith Creek, Mich.

NICKEL GRABBER—Streetcar conductor

NIGGERHEAD—Turret at top of locomotive boiler, over crown sheet, from which saturated steam is taken for operation of pumps, stoker, injectors, and headlight turbine

19 ORDER—Train order that does not have to be signed for. Operator can hand it on a hoop or delivery fork as the train slows down. (See 31 *order*)

99—Failure to protect your train or to flag it

NO-BILL—Nonunion or nonbrotherhood railroad worker. Also called *nonair*

NOSE ON—Couple on with head end of engine

NOSEBAG—Lunch carried to work. *Put on the nosebag* means to eat a meal

NUMBER DUMMY—Yard clerk or car clerk; also called *number grabber*

NUT SPLITTER or NUT BUSTER—Machinist

NUT SPLITTER—A machinist working in the railroad shops.

OILCAN—Tank car

OLD GIRL—Affectionate term for steam engine

OLD HAND—Experienced railroader. Also called *old head*

OLD MAN—Superintendent or general manager

OLE HOSS—Salvage warehouse, or freight on hand

ON THE ADVERTISED—According to schedule; right on time. Often called *on the card* (timecard) and sometimes *on the cat hop*

ON THE CARPET—Commoner version of *dancing on the carpet*

ON THE GROUND—On the ties, as a derailed train

ON THE SPOT—See *spot*

OP—Telegraph operator

OPEN-AIR NAVIGATOR—Hobo riding freight on top

OPEN THE GATE—Switch a train onto or off a siding. *Close the gate* means to close the switch after the train has passed it

O.R.C.—Conductor. (See *big O*)

ORDER BOARD—See *board*

OS—On (train) sheet; to report a train by to dispatcher

OUT—When a trainman is at a point other than his home terminal, either on or off duty, he is *out*

OUTLAWED—See *dogcatchers*

OVER THE KNOLL—Getting up the hill

OVERLAP—Where two block signals control the same stretch of track

OWL—Streetcar or train that runs late at night; almost anything having to do with night

PADDLE—Semaphore signal

PADDLE WHEEL—Narrow-gauge locomotive with driving boxes outside of the wheels

PAIR OF PLIERS—Conductor's punch

PALACE—Caboose

PAPER CAR—Baggage car for the transportation of newspapers exclusively

PAPERWEIGHT—Railroad clerk, office worker. Also called *pencil pusher*

PARLOR—Caboose. *Parlor man* or *parlor maid* is hind brakeman or flagman on freight train

PASSING THE CROAKER—Being examined by company doctor

PEAKED END—Head end of train. Also *pointed* or *sharp end*

PEANUT ROASTER—Any small steam engine

PECK—Twenty minutes allowed for lunch

PEDDLE—To set out freight cars

PEDDLER—Local way-freight train

PELICAN POND—Place outside a roundhouse (down South) where there is much ooze and slime, caused by the fact that many locomotives are run thirty days without the boilers being washed out. The boilers are kept clean by blowing them out with blowoff cocks

PENNSYLVANIA—Coal

PERSUADER—Blower (for locomotive fire)

PETTICOAT—Portion of the exhaust stack that guides exhausted steam into the stack proper. When this becomes displaced, the spent steam goes back through the flues, cutting off the draft from the fire

PIE-CARD—Meal ticket. Also called *grazing ticket*

PIG—Locomotive. *Pig-mauler* is locomotive engineer; *pigpen* locomotive roundhouse. (See *hog*)

PIKE—Railroad

PIN AHEAD AND PICK UP TWO BEHIND ONE—Cut off the engine, pick up three cars from siding, put two on the train, and set the first one back on the siding

PIN FOR HOME—Go home for the day

PINHEAD—Brakeman. *Pin-lifter* is yard brakeman. *Pinner* is a switchman that follows. *Pin-puller* is a switchman that cuts off cars from a train. The old-style link-and-pin coupler was called *Lincoln pin*

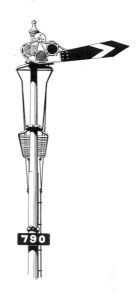

PADDLE—A semaphore signal consisting of a moving arm by day and colored lights by night.

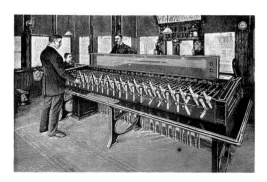

PLANT — An interlocking apparatus used to operate switches and signals from a single location. The plant was located in a railroad yard or terminal.

PINK—Caution card or rush telegram

PLANT—Interlocking system

PLUG—"One-horse" passenger train. Also throttle of old-style locomotive; hence engineers were known as *plug-pullers. Plugging her* means using the reverse lever as a brake instead of the air. Local passenger trains are sometimes referred to as *plug runs*

PLUSH RUN—Passenger train

POCATELLO YARDMASTER—Derisive term for *boomers,* all of whom presumably claimed to have held, at some time, the tough job of night yardmaster at Pocatello, Idaho

POLE—To *run light.* (See *light*)

POLE PIN—Superintendent of telegraph

POP—To let safety valve on boiler release, causing waste of steam, making a loud noise, and, when engine is working hard, raising water in boiler, thereby causing locomotive to work water

POP CAR—Gasoline car or *speeder,* used by section men, linemen, etc.; so called because of the put-put noise of its motor exhaust

POPS—*Retainers*

POSITIVE BLOCK—Locomotive engineer

POSSUM BELLY—Toolbox under a caboose or under some wrecking cars

POUND HER—Work a locomotive to its full capacity

POUNDING THEIR EARS—Sleeping, *making hay*

PUD—Pick up and delivery service

PULLER—Switch engine hauling cars from one yard to another at the same terminal. Also the operator of an electric truck that transfers baggage and mail around a terminal

PULL FREIGHT—To leave or to give up a job

PULL THE AIR—Set brakes by opening conductor's valve or angle cock

PULL THE CALF'S TAIL—Yank the whistle cord

PULL THE PIN—Uncouple a car by pulling up the coupling pin. A *boomer* expression meaning to resign or quit a job

PURE-FOOD LAW—See *dogcatchers*

PUSHER—Extra engine on rear of train, usually placed there to assist in climbing a grade

PUSSYFOOTER—Railroad policeman

PUT 'ER ON—Make a reduction in air in the train's braking system. *Put 'er all on* means apply emergency brake, more commonly described as *big-holing her*

PUT ON THE NOSEBAG—Eat a meal

QUILL—Whistle (term used especially in the South)

QUILLING—Personalized technique of blowing a locomotive whistle, applicable only in the days before the whistles became standardized

RABBIT—A derail; an arrangement for preventing serious wrecks by sidetracking runaway trains, cars, or locomotives on a downgrade. Unlike regular sidetracks, the derail ends relatively abruptly on flat trackless land instead of curving back onto the main line. The term *rabbit* is applied to this device because of the timidity involved

RACE TRACK—Straight and flat stretch of track upon which an en-

RABBIT — A derail, or a type of switch which would sidetrack a runaway train or car. Unlike most switches, the derail ended abruptly on trackless land.

gineer can safely make unusually high speed. Also parallel stretches of track of two competing railroads upon which rival trains race one another (contrary to company rules but much to the delight of enginemen, trainmen, and passengers, and perhaps to the secret delight of some officials)

RAG-WAVER—Flagman

RAIL—Any railroad employee

RAILFAN—Anyone who makes a hobby of railroading

RAP THE STACK—Give your locomotive a wide-open throttle, make more speed. *Rapper* is an engineer who works his engine too hard

RATTLE HER HOCKS—Get speed out of an engine

RATTLER—Freight train

RAWHIDER—Official, or any employee, who is especially hard on men or equipment, or both, with which he works. A *rawhider*, or *slave driver*, delights in causing someone to do more than his share of work. Running too fast when picking up a man on the footboard, or making a quick stop just short of him when he is expecting to step on, so that he has to walk back, are two ways it is done; but there are almost as many ways of *rawhiding* as there are different situations

REAL ESTATE—Poor coal mixed with dirt or slag. When mixed with sand it is called *seashore*

RED BOARD—Stop signal

REDBALL, BALL OF FIRE—Fast freight train, *hotshot*

REDCAP—Station porter. Term coined about 1900 by George H. Daniels, New York Central publicist

RED EYE—Same as *red board*; also liquor

RED ONION—Eating house or sleeping quarters for railroad men

REEFER or RIFF—Refrigerator car

REPTILE—See *snake*

RETAINER—Small valve located near brake wheel for drawing off and holding air on cars. (*Retainers* often figure prominently in true tales and fiction stories about runaway cars on trains)

RIDIN' 'EM HIGH—Traveling on tops of boxcars

RIDIN' THE RODS—An old-time hobo practice, now virtually obsolete. The hobo would place a board across truss rods under a car and ride on it. This was very dangerous even in pleasant weather, and the possibility was ever present that you might doze, get careless, become too cramped, or lose your nerve—and roll under the wheels

RIDING THE POINT—Riding a locomotive, *point* referring to shape of pilot

RIGHT-HAND SIDE—Engineer's side of cab (on nearly all North American roads). Left-hand side is fireman's side. When a fireman is promoted he is *set up to the right-hand side*

RINGMASTER—Yardmaster

RIPRAP—Loose pieces of heavy stone or masonry used in some places to protect roadbeds from water erosion

RIP-TRACK—Minor repair track or car-repair department. *Rip* means repair

RIVET BUSTER—Boilermaker

ROAD HOG—Any large motor vehicle on a highway, especially intercity trailer trucks and busses that cut into railroad freight and passenger revenue

RAG-WAVER—A flagman who protected the rear of a train or railroad crossing.

RUNT—A dwarf semaphore or small color signal.

ROOFED—Caught in close clearance

ROOF GARDEN—Mallet-type locomotive or any helper engine on a mountain job. Sometimes called *sacred ox*

ROUGHNECK—Freight brakeman

RUBBERNECK CAR—Observation car

RULE G—"The use of intoxicants or narcotics is prohibited"—one of twelve general rules in standard code adopted by Association of American Railroads, based upon previous regulations made by individual companies. Countless thousands of railroad men, especially *boomers*, have been discharged for violation of *Rule G;* not because of railroads' objection to liquor itself but because a man under the influence of liquor is not to be trusted in a job involving human lives and property

RUN—The train to which a man is assigned is his *run*

RUN-AROUND—If it is a man's turn to work and he is not called, he may claim pay for the work he missed. He has been given the *run-around*

RUN-IN—A collision; an argument or fight

RUN LIGHT—For an engine to run on the tracks without any cars

RUNNER—Locomotive engineer

RUNT—Dwarf signal

RUST or STREAK O' RUST—Railroad

RUST PILE—Old locomotive

RUSTLING THE BUMS—Searching a freight train for hobos. In bygone days it was common practice for trainmen to collect money from freight-riding *'bos*, often at the rate of a dollar a division

SADDLE—First stop of freight car, under the lowest grab iron

SANDHOG—Laborer who works in a caisson tunneling under a river, boring either a railroad tunnel, subway, or highway tunnel

SAP—Same as *brake club;* also called *the staff of ignorance*. To set hand brakes is to *sap up some binders*

SAWBONES—Company doctor

SAW BY—Slow complicated operation whereby one train passes another on a single-track railroad when the other is on a siding too short to hold the entire train. *Saw by* is applied to any move through switches or through connecting switches that is necessitated by one train passing another

SCAB—Nonunion workman; also car not equipped with automatic air system. (See *nonair*)

SCIZZOR-BILL—Uncomplimentary term referring to yard or road brakemen and students in train service

SCOOP—Fireman's shovel. Also the step on front and rear ends of switch engines

SCOOT—Shuttle train

SCRAP PILE—Worn-out locomotive that is still in service

SEAT HOG—Passenger who monopolizes more than one seat in a car or station waiting room while others are standing. Such pests usually spread luggage, packages, or lunch over adjacent seats

SEASHORE—Sand used in sand dome. Also applied to coal that is mixed with sand

SECRET WORKS—Automatic air-brake application. Also the draft

RUSTLING THE BUMS — Searching the train for hoboes. In days gone by, trainmen would rustle the bums for a small fee in payment for their passage over a railroad division.

timbers and drawbar of a car, when extracted by force. If only the drawbar is pulled out, you say, "We got a lung," but if the draft timbers come with it, you say, "We got the whole damn secret works"

SENIORITY GRABBER—Railroad employee who is glad when someone above him dies, gets killed, is fired, or resigns, so he can move up the seniority list to a better job

SEPARATION—The sorting of mail sacks and parcels within the storage car before transferring to trucks

SERVICE APPLICATION—Gradual speed reduction, as contrasted with emergency stop caused by *wiping the clock*

SETTING UP—Loading a baggage car with mail and parcels according to a prearranged plan to facilitate rapid unloading at various stations along the line

SETUP—Four to six hand trucks placed in formation beside the door of a storage car to facilitate the separation of the mail and parcels being unloaded. Each truck is loaded with matter to be transferred to other trains or to the R.P.O. (Railway Post Office) terminal office

SHACK—Brakeman, occupant of caboose. *Shack's master* is a conductor

SHAKE 'EM UP—Switching

SHAKING THE TRAIN—Putting on air brakes in emergency

SHANTY—Caboose

SHINER—Brakeman's or switchman's lantern

SHINING TIME—Starting time (probably from old Negro spiritual "Rise and Shine")

SHOO-FLY—Temporary track, usually built around a flooded area, a wreck, or other obstacle; sometimes built merely to facilitate a re-railing

SHORT FLAGGING—Flagman not far enough from his train to protect it. (See *drawbar flagging*)

SHORT LOADS—Cars consigned to points between division points and set out on sidings at their destinations. Also called *shorts*

SHORT-TIME CREW—Crew working overtime but not yet affected by the sixteen-hour law. (See *dogcatchers*)

SHUFFLE THE DECK—Switch cars onto house tracks at every station you pass on your run

SHUNTING BOILER—Switch engine

SIDE-DOOR PULLMAN—Boxcar used by hobos in stealing rides

SKATE—Shoe placed on rail in hump yard to stop cars with defective brakes

SKIN YOUR EYE—Engineer's warning to man on left side of cab when approaching curve

SKIPPER—Conductor

SKYROCKETS—Red-hot cinders from smokestack

SLAVE DRIVER—Yardmaster. Also any *rawhider*

SLING MORSE—Work as telegraph operator

SLIPS, CAR OR TRAIN OF—Car or train of bananas

SLOW BOARD—See *board*

SLUG—Heavy fire in locomotive firebox

SLUGS—A shipment of magazines, catalogues, or automobile-license plates in small mail sacks weighing approximately 100 pounds each

SMART ALECK—Passenger conductor

SEPARATION—Sorting the mail and parcels within the mail or storage car.

SNOOZER — The name given to the Pullman sleeping car by railroad men.

SPEEDER — A car used to carry a small group of railroad men. In the early days, the speeder carried a small kerosene boiler rather than the gasoline engine of today.

SMOKE or SMOKE AGENT—Locomotive fireman. *Smoker* is engine or firebox. *Smoking 'em* or *running on smoke orders* is a dangerous method, now obsolete, of running a train from one station or siding to another without orders from the dispatcher. You moved cautiously, continually watching for the smoke of any train that might be approaching you on the same track

SNAKE—Switchman, so named from the large serpentine letter S on membership pins of the Switchman's Union of North America. Sometimes called *reptile* or *serpent*

SNAKEHEAD—A rail that comes loose from the ties and pierces the floor of a car; a fairly common accident with the strap-iron rails of a century ago

SNAP—Push or pull with another engine. *Snapper* is the engine that does the pulling

SNIPE—Track laborer. His boss is a *king snipe*

SNOOZER—Pullman sleeping car

SNUFF DIPPERS—Coal-burning engines that burn lignite (which, on the Missouri Pacific at least, is the same color as snuff)

SOAK—Saturated locomotive

SODA JERKER—Locomotive fireman

SOFT BELLIES—Wooden frame cars

SOFT-DIAMOND SPECIAL—Coal train

SOFT PLUG—Fusible plug in crown sheet of locomotive that is supposed to drop when water gets below top of sheet

SOLID CAR—A completely filled storage car containing sixty feet of mail and parcels, equal to a 100 per cent load

SOLID TRACK—Track full of cars

SPAR—Pole used to shove cars into the clear when switching. (See *stake*)

SPEED GAUGER—Locomotive engineer

SPEEDER—Same as *pop car*

SPEEDY—Callboy

SPIKE A TORCH—Throw a *fusee*

SPOT—To place a car in a designated position. Also sleep, rest, or lunch period on company time. *On the spot* means an opportunity for railroad men to "chew the rag" or swap experiences. Unlike the same underworld term, *on the spot* has no sinister implication in railroad slang

SPOTBOARD—Guide used by section men in surfacing or ballasting track in order to obtain an even bed.

SPOTTER—Spy, company man assigned to snoop around and check on employees

SQUEEZERS—Car-retarding system used in some railroad *yards*

SQUIRRELING—Climbing a car

STACK O' RUST—A locomotive that has seen better days

STAKE—Pole used in dangerous and now rare method of switching. A cut of cars was shoved by a *stake* attached to the car immediately in front of the engine. This method was supposed to be superior to the ordinary method of "batting them out" because there was less wear and tear on drawbars and less damage to freight; but the human casualties that resulted gave more than one *yard* the nickname "slaughterhouse." Another meaning of *stake* is the money a *boomer* saved on a job so he could resign and continue eating regularly while looking for another job

STAKE DRIVER—Any engineering-department man

STALL—Space inside a mail or baggage car containing mail or parcels consigned to a certain destination and separated from other shipments by removable steel posts

STARGAZER—Brakeman who fails to see signals

STARVATION DIET—See *board*

STEM—Track or right-of-way

STEM-WINDER—Climax type of geared locomotive. Also applied to trolley car without brakes because of the motion of its brake handle

STICK—Staff used on certain stretches of track to control the block. It is carried by engine crews from one station to another. Now rare

STIFF BUGGY—Specially designed four-wheel truck used for transferring coffins and rough boxes inside a station

STINGER—Brakeman. Derived from initial B(ee) of Brotherhood of Railroad Trainmen, or perhaps from some brakemen's habit of arousing hobos by applying a brake club to the soles of their shoes

STINK BUGGY—Bus

STINKER—Hotbox

STIRRUP—First step of freight car, under the lowest *grab iron*

STOCK PEN—Yard office

STOCKHOLDER—Any employee who is always looking out for the company's interests

STOPPER PULLER—Member of the crew that follows the engine in switching

STORAGE CAR—Baggage car or (in rush periods) Railway Express car containing a mixed shipment of parcels and mail sacks consigned to a certain terminal for sorting and rerouting to various destinations via other trains

STRAW BOSS—Foreman of small gang or acting foreman

STRAW-HAT BOYS—Railroad men who work only in pleasant weather

STRAWBERRY PATCH—Rear end of caboose by night; also railroad yard studded with red lights

STRETCH 'EM OUT—Take out slack in couplings and drawbars of train

STRING—Several cars coupled together; also a telegraph wire

STRUGGLE FOR LIFE—Existence in railroad boardinghouse

STUDE TALLOW—Student fireman

STUDENT—Learner in either telegraph, train, or engine service; an apprentice

SUCK IT BY—Make a *flying switch*

SUGAR—Sand

SUPER—Superintendent

SWELLHEAD—Conductor or locomotive engineer

SWING A BUG—Make a good job of braking. (See *bug*)

SWING MAN—Same as *middle man*

SWITCH LIST—Bill of fare at railroad eating house

SWITCH MONKEY—Switchman

SWITCH MONKEY — A switchman who switched cars within a yard or terminal.

TAIL OVER HER BACK—Engine with full head of steam, with plume resembling a squirrel's tail from her safety valve

TAKE THE RUBBER OUT OF THEM—Disconnect the air hoses on a train

TAKING YOUR MINUTES—Stopping for lunch

TALLOWPOT—Locomotive fireman, so called from melted tallow used to lubricate valves and shine the engine

TANK—Locomotive tender. *Tanker* is tank car used in hauling oil, water, milk, chemicals or some other liquid

TEAKETTLE—See *kettle*

TELLTALES—Any device that serves as a warning. Specifically the row of strips hanging down a short distance in front of a tunnel or low bridge to inform trainmen who are riding car tops that they'd better duck

TERMINAL—Railway Post Office unit, usually at or near the railroad station, where mail is removed from sacks, sorted, and forwarded to its ultimate destination

TERMINAL LOAD—A shipment of mail consigned to a certain R.P.O. terminal office for sorting and reshipment in other sacks

TEASE THE BRUTE—Follow the engine

THE BISCUITS HANG HIGH—There's a scarcity of food handouts in that locality

THIRTY—Telegraphic term for "that's all—no more"

31 ORDER—Train order that must be signed for; the train must stop to pick it up. (See 19 *order*)

THOUSAND-MILER—Black satin or blue percale shirt worn by railroaders, expected to last 1,000 miles between washings. (The usual basis of a day's work was about 100 miles, so two shirts could easily last from one pay day to the next)

THREE-BAGGER—Train pushed or pulled by three engines. (No doubt originated by a baseball fan)

THROTTLE-JERKER—Engineer

THROW AWAY THE DIAMONDS—Term applied to locomotive fireman missing the firedoor with a shovelful of coal and spilling some

TIE 'EM DOWN—Set handbrakes

TIE ON—Couple on. *Tie 'em together* is to couple cars

TIE UP—Stop for a meal or for rest

TIER—Pile of mail sacks or parcels occupying the full width at each end of a car

TIMKENIZED—Equipped with Timken roller bearings

TIN LIZARD—Streamlined train

TING-A-LING—Small engine with "tinny" bell

TISSUE—Train order. (See *flimsy*)

TOAD—Derail. (See *rabbit*)

TOEPATH or TOWPATH—Running board of locomotive or *catwalk* on top of boxcars, or that part of railroad embankment lying between end of ties and shoulders of *fill*

TONK—Car repairer

TONNAGE HOUND—Trainmaster or other official who insists upon

TIE 'EM DOWN — To set handbrakes. The position of brakeman was one of peculiar hardship and peril, especially in winter when he had to stand without shelter and expose himself to the elements.

longer or heavier trains than the crew and motive power can handle efficiently

TOP DRESSER DRAWER—Upper bunk in caboose

TOWER BUFF—*Railfan* so zealous that he disregards signs such as "Private," "No Admittance" and "Stay Out" on interlocking towers and other railroad structures

TRAIN LINE—Pipe that carries compressed air to operate air brakes

TRAMPIFIED—The way a *boomer* looked after being out of work a long time. His clothes were "ragged as a barrel of sauerkraut" and he needed a "dime's worth of decency" (shave)

TRAVELING CARD—Card given by a railroad Brotherhood to a man in search of employment. Also an empty slip bill

TRAVELING GRUNT—Road foreman of engines, traveling engineer. Sometimes called *traveling man*

TRICK—Shift, hours of duty

TRIMMER—Engine working in *hump yard* that goes down into *yard* and picks out misdirected cars and shoves them to clear. (See *yard* and *hump*)

TWO-WHEELER—Two-wheeled hand truck for transferring baggage and mail around in a station

UNCLE SAM—Railway Post Office clerk

UNDER THE TABLE—Just as a man who "can't take his liquor" is sometimes actually *under the table*, so, figuratively, is a telegraph operator when messages are being sent to him faster than he can receive

UNDERGROUND HOG—Chief engineer

UNLOAD—Get off train hurriedly

VARNISH—Passenger train. Also called *varnished shot, varnished job, varnished boxes, string of varnish, varnished wagons,* etc. These nicknames are rarely applied to modern streamliners

VASELINE—Oil

WABASH—To hit cars going into adjacent tracks. (See *cornered*) Also refers to the officially frowned-upon practice of slowing up for a stop signal at a crossing with another railroad instead of stopping. The engineer would look up and down to make sure everything is safe, then start up again, having saved several minutes by not stopping entirely. *Wabash* may also mean a heavy fire in the locomotive firebox

WAGON—Railroad car. (English term)

WALK THE DOG—Wheel a freight so fast as to make cars sway from side to side

WALK UP AGAINST THE GUN—Ascend a steep grade with the injector on

WALL STREET NOTCH—Forward corner of reverse lever quadrant in engine cab (more commonly called *company notch*). Called *Wall Street notch* because engine pays dividends when heaviness of train requires engine to be worked that way

WASHOUT—Stop signal, waved violently by using both arms and

UNCLE SAM — Name given to the Railway Post Office crews who were government employees rather than railroad men.

VARNISH — A passenger train was often called the varnish or string of varnish. When cars were made of wood, a heavy coat of varnish was applied on top of the paint to protect it. This gave the cars a slick or polished appearance. Passengers of a high class train were "riding the varnish".

swinging them in downward arc by day, or swinging lamp in wide low semicircle across tracks at night

WATCH YOUR PINS—Be careful around stacks of ties, rails, etc.

WAY CAR—Caboose, or car of local freight

WEARING THE BLUE—Delayed by car inspectors. A blue flag or blue light is placed on cars thus delayed and being worked on

WEARING THE GREEN—Carrying green signals. When trains run in more than one section, all except the last must display two green flags

WEED BENDER—Railroaders' derisive term for cowboy, other such terms being *hay shaker*, *clover picker*, and *plow jockey*. Commonest term for cowboy is *cowpuncher*, which is of railroad origin. Cowboys riding stock trains prod the cattle

WESTINGHOUSE—Air brake, also called *windjammer*

WET MULE IN THE FIREBOX—Bad job of firing a locomotive

WHALE BELLY—Steel car, or type of coal car with drop bottom. Also called *sow belly*

WHEEL 'EM—Let a train run without braking. *Wheeling* means carrying or hauling at good speed; also called *highballing*. You say *wheeling the berries* when you mean hauling the berry crop at high speed

WHEEL 'EM — Rolling a train at good speed without applying the brakes.

WHEEL MONKEY—Car inspector

WHEN DO YOU SHINE?—What time were you called for?

WHISKERS—Quite a bit of seniority

WHISTLE OUT A FLAG—Engineer blows one long and three short blasts for the brakeman to protect rear of train

WHITE FEATHER—Plume of steam over safety valves, indicating high boiler pressure

WHITE RIBBONS—White flags (an extra train)

WHITEWASH—Milk

WIDEN ON HER—Open the throttle, increase speed

WIGWAG—A grade-crossing signal

WILLIE—Waybill for loaded car

WIND—Air brakes

WING HER—Set brakes on moving train

WISE GUY—Station agent

WOLF or LONE WOLF—Nonbrotherhood man

WORKING A CAR—Unloading a storage mail car

WORKING MAIL—Mail in sacks and pouches consigned to R.P.O. (Railway Post Office) cars to be "worked" or sorted in transit

WORK WATER—Some old-time engineers preferred to *work the water* (operate the injector and watch the water glass or gauge cocks). On most roads the fireman now *works the water*

WRECKING CREW—Relief crew. Derogatory term derived from the difficulty regular men sometimes experience in rearranging a car after it has been used by relief men

WRONG IRON—Main track on which the current of traffic is in the opposite direction

WYE—Tracks running off the main line or *lead*, forming a letter Y; used for turning cars and engines where no turntable is available

X—Empty car

XXX—Same as *bad order*

YARD—System of tracks for making up trains or storing cars. (*Boomer's* version: "System of *rust* surrounded by fence and inhabited by a dumb bunch of natives who will not let a train in or out.") Also called *garden* and *field*. *Yard geese* are yard switchmen. Y.M. is yardmaster. *Yard goat* is switching engine

ZOO KEEPER—Gate tender at passenger station

ZULU CAR — During the homesteading days on the Western plains, the term applied to a boxcar which transported an immigrant, his family, household goods, farm equipment, and livestock all in one car. The expression derived from the carload of polygamous Zulu warriors, their families, and possessions that toured the United States with the Barnum & Bailey Circus in the 1880's. These fierce African tribesmen aroused much public interest since their King Cetewayo inflicted a major defeat to the proud British Army at Isandhlwana.

ZULU — Emigrant families crossing the plains in the 1880's rode in little more than a box car. The tay was wet and pipe-smoke often mingled with garlic.

BALING-WIRE REPAIRS — One of the happier incidents that brought respite to train-weary passengers was a breakdown on the road in picturesque countryside. While crews made repairs as best they could, passengers wandered idly or offered advice on how to remedy the situation.

Last of the Birneys

by
E. S. Peyton and R. A. Moorman

— AL ROSE

THE HEYDEY of the trolley car may be over, but who doesn't remember the singing sound of the trolley wire, the rumble of traction motors, the cheerful voice of the motorman as he calls the stops, and the clang-clang of the bell? For each of us, the street car will remain a cherished part of our American heritage.

Fort Collins was by no means the first city in the state of Colorado to have a street railway line, but it has gone down in the annals of Colorado history as the last. In its enduring days, the Fort Collins Municipal Railway was one of the most fascinating and unique street railway systems in the United States. Its dinky Birney type trolleys, all dressed in silver and red livery, bobbed along the tree lined streets of this agricultural and college center. Aficionados, electric railway historians, and photographers armed with more than one camera, flocked into Fort Collins from all corners of the world. The story of this remarkable little railway is full of civic struggle and accomplishment.

67

In 1906, the city council of Fort Collins granted a franchise to the Denver & Interurban Railroad, a subsidiary of the Colorado & Southern Railway, for the construction and operation of street car lines on certain streets within the city. The C&S was at this time an important unit in the transportation system of Colorado, especially the northern part of the state. Contrary to the policy of most steam operated railroads, the C&S was interested in local transportation systems of towns served by its steam lines. Under its subsidiary company the Denver & Interurban, the C&S owned a half interest in the electric division of the Colorado Springs & Cripple Creek District Railway. This line serves the mines of the fabulous gold camps of Cripple Creek and Victor. A proposed electric railway connecting Denver, Boulder, Longmont, Loveland and Fort Collins was on the drawing boards. Though its various electric properties were widely separated, they were connected by the steam railroad lines of the parent company. If the automobile had not changed the American transportation picture in such haste, this system might well have reached from Cripple Creek to Cheyenne, Wyoming. There was some speculation at the time that an extension to the great steel mills of Pueblo was in the offing.

The first step in the construction of the D&I was the development of a city system in Fort Collins. The *Fort Collins Express* noted that "Work on the street railway will begin in earnest on next Tuesday (July 9, 1907)." On that day a large steam traction engine began plowing up West Mountain Avenue in preparation for the actual work of laying track. Enough rails and ties were on hand for about four blocks of track. Second-hand steel from the C&S main line was obtained. A new carbarn and power house were under construction at the corner of Howes and Cherry Streets. Newspapers expressed some concern that College Avenue would be "spoiled by the construction of a street car line on its much driven surface." In spite of high wages ($1.65 a day) labor was scarce. Workmen were recruited in Denver, and the line progressed rapidly into the winter months.

One of the events of the year was the annual Race Meet and Stock Show, held during August. In 1907 local advertisements appeared in the papers saying: "Everyone should attend the Race Meet and Stock Show, August 28, 29, and 30. Street Car Service all the way." This, in spite of the fact that the power plant had not been completed, track work had barely been started and not a single car had been purchased. In order to

carry out this promise, the C&S built a temporary transfer track across the Court House lawn to the D&I track on West Mountain Avenue. Track was completed to the fair grounds at Prospect Park and a small steam locomotive No. 203, an 0-6-0 type, and four ancient open platform wooden coaches were used to carry pasengers to the Race Meet.

Clyde Brown of the Fort Collins Pioneer Museum, remembers riding this train. The *Fort Collins Express* of August 29, 1907, gave the following account of the operation:

"By far the greatest portion of the people were taken to the grounds by means of the steam cars which were run by the C&S in lieu of street cars which it was impossible to secure electricity for at the present time. When the first train pulled out to the fair grounds in the morning a great deal of interest was shown by all concerned. Officials of the road and citizens of the city, packed the train with passengers. Conductor William Hill had control of the train, Engineer Walter Hayes and Fireman E. Kirkpatrick were in the cab, and B. L. Collins and C. A. Wilfong collected the nickels. The engine, Number 203, had just been brought from Denver where it had received a thorough rejuvenation."

The train ran west on Mountain Avenue to the fair grounds, then backed-up to the starting point. It ran the three days of the fair. Although there was some disappointment at the use of a steam train, the papers noted that: "The use of the heavier train had a tendency to help settle the track." This train operated every half hour, and business was good. The fare, as provided by the street railway franchise, was five cents. After the fair closed the train was returned to the C&S and the transfer track removed.

By early December 1907, the Fort Collins City Lines of the D&I were about ready for use. The *Express* states that: "Power has been turned on at the new power house of the Denver & Interurban Railway, and the machines are running every day. The machines will have 400 horsepower each. All the trolley wires are in place and are ready for use and little remains to complete the system. An official of the road said Thursday that some cars will be run out on the track, most any day now, but that the road could not be put in operation before two weeks, and the schedule would not be in force before January 1st."

Several trips were made to instruct motormen and, prior to Christmas 1907, the company issued a statement to the papers outlining details gov-

Painted in Brewster green with gold striping, motor M-104 pauses for a classic builder's illustration at the Woeber Carriage Works of Denver, Colorado. At the right, motor M-102 loaded on a flat car enroute to Fort Collins. — BOTH R. H. KINDIG COLLECTION

erning operations and schedules that were to be in effect following a dedication trip on December 29, 1907.

OPERATIONS OF CARS AND SCHEDULES

"Cars will leave the intersection of College and Mountain Avenues at 5:30 A.M., returning to the C&S depot at 6:10 to give passengers for the early morning train time to purchase tickets and check baggage before departure. Beginning at 6:20 cars will depart every twenty minutes, that is, at 6:20, 6:40, 7:00, 7:20, 7:40, and 8:00, keeping up this schedule until 11:20 P.M. Cars will stop to receive and discharge passengers at the further side of street crossings. College Avenue cars and Mountain Avenue cars will run over the loop, that is, they will continue down College Avenue to Jefferson Street, around Jefferson to Linden Street, back on Linden to the intersection of College and Mountain Avenues. Transfers will be issued at the intersection of Mountain and College Avenues to passengers wishing to continue on either line. Passengers should ask for these transfers when paying their fares to the conductor. Children under six years of age, when accompanied by a paying passenger, will be carried free of charge. Children over six years of age and under twelve years of age will be carried at half fare. Conductors will be provided with half-fare tickets at the rate of ten for twenty-five cents."

Two lines were placed in operation, and two cars operated the base service. Additional cars were added when needed.

The College Avenue line ran south on College Avenue past Colorado A&M College to Pitkin Street, east on Pitkin to Remington (one block) and then north on Remington to Elizabeth Street (three blocks), then back to College Avenue. The Mountain Avenue line ran straight west on Mountain Avenue for 20 blocks to the cemetery where there was a small loop and a shelter for passengers.

The *Express* gave an interesting account of the dedication of the new road. "The cars are of a modern type superior in many respects to those in use in Denver. They are new, clean and comfortable.

Three generations of land transportation are gathered at Lindenmeier Lake. The dance hall and pavillion were located a short distance behind the trolley, while the lake itself was on the left out of sight. — J. O. Beeler Collection

Looking south on College Avenue about 1910. Note the two trolley cars operating on the left hand track against the flow of vehicles. — Steve Maguire Collection

The equipment at the power plant is adequate. All the citizens who enjoyed the dedication ride were pleased with what they saw, and pronounced everything to their liking. Mr. Parker (Vice-President of the C&S) was delighted and showed his pleasure like a boy of 16 years."

The motor cars were built by the Woeber Carriage Works of Denver, Colorado, car builder for the Denver Tramway Corporation. They were double-truck, double-end, monitor deck wooden cars with open platforms and equipped with air brakes. Capacity was 44 passengers and each car weighed 40,000 pounds. The trolleys were painted Brewster green with gold lettering and striping.

Scheduled operations began December 29, 1907, and Fort Collins became a "Street Car Town". In 1908 a line was built to Lindenmeier Lake, a resort some two and one-half miles from the city. A pavilion was erected, boat landings were built and the lake became well-known as a summer recreation spot. Trolley service made it easy for the people of Fort Collins to spend an evening dancing or a pleasant Sunday afternoon boating on the lake. The Lindenmeier Lake line was combined with the College Avenue line, two cars being used in base service, and they passed each other on the downtown loop. Since the Lindenmeier Lake car was often late, a hand-operated semaphore was installed at the corner of Jefferson and Linden Streets, governing the outbound car. Inbound cars came straight down Linden Street to the intersection of College and Mountain Avenues, while outbound cars went north on College Avenue to Jefferson Street, and then east to Linden Street, then north toward the lake. Some fast running was necessary on the Lindenmeier Lake line as cars made the round trip in 20 minutes. On holidays and weekends trolleys were packed on this line and extras were often run.

There was some agitation on the part of the Country Club directors located a mile north of Lindenmeier Lake to have the line extended to the club's grounds. This the company was willing to do provided the club would bear part of the expense of building the extension, and if the club would guarantee a certain precentage of business. Since a bridge was necessary over a large irrigation ditch, and the cost of the extension would be around $20,-000, the club was either unwilling or unable to assure responsibility for the project and the idea "died a 'borning".

In the summer of 1909, street car No. 106 struck and completely cut in half a large Russian Wolfhound. The *Express* noted editorially; "The death of the dog itself is unimportant in comparison to the lesson it teaches in regard to the danger of the cars equipped as they are with ineffective fenders

for the protection of life. —WHAT WOULD HAP-
PEN TO THE CHILDREN?" The paper also
stated: "The fenders in use were some eight or
nine inches above the rail, but when cars were
heavily loaded they sometimes touched the rails."
Conductor Beeler stated in 1957 that he believes
this to be inaccurate. The only place he recalls
fenders or pilots touching the rails was at the C&S
steam railroad crossing on West Mountain Avenue.
Here the track was not always well maintained,
and often rough.

For the most part, the people of Fort Collins
were satisfied with their trolley system and considerable local pride was shown in the numerous
articles appearing in local newspapers. The *Fort
Collins Courier* published a semi-centennial edition
in 1914 which carried this article:

FORT COLLINS STREET CAR SYSTEM EQUAL TO METROPOLITAN IN EQUIPMENT AND SERVICE

"The Fort Collins street Car System is equal
in every respect to the best metropolitan street
railroad and is always the cause of comment
by visitors to the city. There are between six
and seven miles of track covering the business
and residence sections of the city and extending to points of interest in the outskirts of the
town. The cars are of the most modern type,
comfortably heated in winter and cool in the
summer. So good is the system and service
maintained in fact, that the system has never
really been a paying proposition and is continued in order to hold the franchise against
the time when the city will have grown to such
proportions as to make the system a paying
one. The system is operated by the Denver &
Interurban Company, a subsidiary to the Colorado & Southern Ry. Co. Twenty men find
steady employment in the service of the company and its payroll amounts to $16,000 an-
nually. The policy of employing only Fort Collins men as pursued by the Railway Company
is followed by the Street Car Company, thus
giving the City twenty substantial citizens,
some owning their own homes and rearing their
families."

In a history of Larimer County published in
1911, an account of the company presents the following favorable comments:

"Built by the Denver & Interurban. City
council granted franchise in 1906. Construction started in summer of 1907 and began operating over five miles of track December 29,
1907. College Avenue; Jefferson to Pitkin to
Remington to Elizabeth, to College Avenue.
Mountain Avenue; Mountain Avenue to Grand

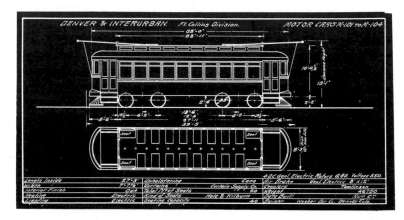

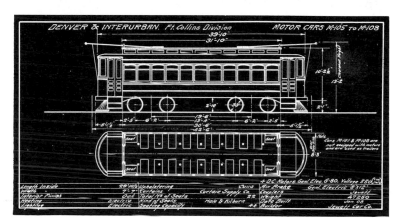

Equipment diagrams with specifications of both
types of Fort Collins trolley cars are reproduced from the pages of the Denver & Interurban Equipment Folio No. 32. Note the
difference between the Woeber motor M-101
to M-104 and the Jewett cars M-105 to M-108.

View Cemetery. Jefferson; from College Ave.
to Mountain Ave. at Peterson. (This is incor-
rect for the line ran down Jefferson Street only
to Linden St. Further extension in 1909 Whedbee Street Line.) In 1908 lines extended past
the Great Western Sugar factory to Lindenmeier Lake. The Company gives twenty minute service on all these lines, and the people of
Fort Collins find the street cars a great con-
venience. The tracks and equipment are first
class in all respects, and the Company is well
managed."

In the years that followed, the Denver & Interurban was just another small town trolley line,
somewhat better than the average. People were
proud of their street car system and patronized it.
Yet there was always criticism of the Lindenmeier
Lake line. Business was good on weekends and holidays, but base weekday traffic was light. As business fell off on this line, schedules were reduced.

Denver & Interurban Railroad

1908-1918

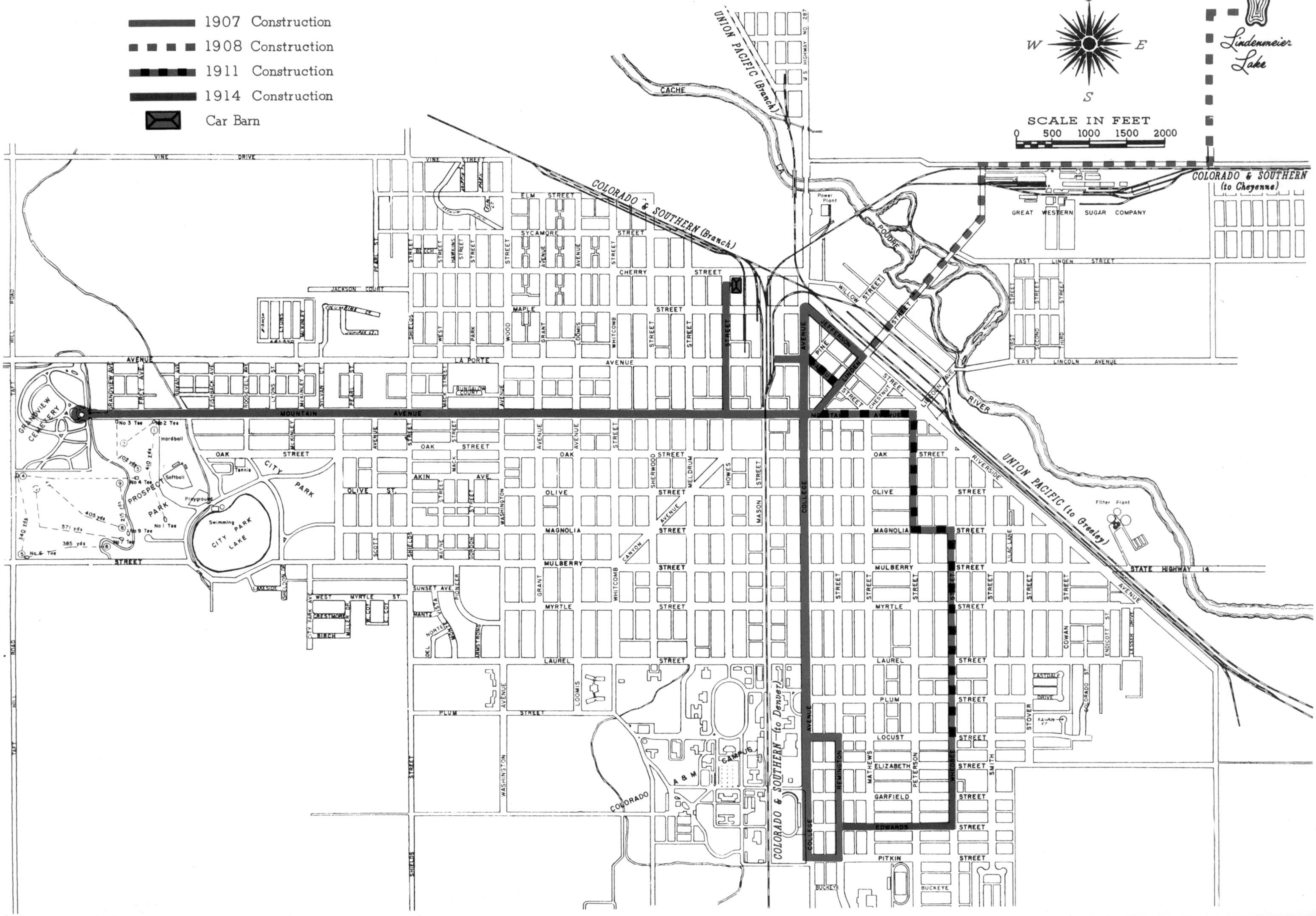

Lindenmeier Lake

SCALE IN FEET
0 500 1000 1500 2000

1907 Construction
1908 Construction
1911 Construction
1914 Construction
Car Barn

COLORADO & SOUTHERN (to Cheyenne)

GREAT WESTERN SUGAR COMPANY

UNION PACIFIC (to Greeley)

STATE HIGHWAY 14

Filter Plant

UNION PACIFIC (Branch)

U.S. HIGHWAY NO. 287

POUDRE RIVER

Power Plant

COLORADO & SOUTHERN (Branch)

COLORADO & SOUTHERN (to Denver)

CACHE LA POUDRE

CITY PARK

CITY PARK LAKE

Swimming Pool
Tennis
Golf

PROSPECT PARK

GRANDVIEW CEMETERY

A & M

Fort Collins trolleymen J. O. Beeler and Bill Williams pose for a crew portrait alongside M-106. — J. O. Beeler Collection

The rapid decline in patronage on some scheduled runs became a nation-wide street railway problem. The average number of passengers carried per car mile during 1912 for most of the smaller traction properties was between four and five. This was also true for the Denver & Interurban. This meant that a car had to travel one-fourth mile for each fare collected. On many trips the crew outnumbered the passengers. On a few runs there were no passengers at all. Small wonder the street railway operators began to question the need for two men on each trolley. One-man operation was a quick solution. This would cut platform expense in half, and one man could keep reasonably busy yet offering efficient service to the rider.

Conversion to one-man operation was simple. The company closed up the back end of the car, and installed a fare box in the front-end under the eye of the motorman. Stops were then changed to the near-side of the cross streets for easier loading. The public believed this a sensible thing to introduce rather than cut service to effect an economy. Management stated, "A single-man car equipped with folding doors and steps, if operated properly, is practically as safe as when operated by two men, and the number of accidents and the amount of damage therefrom does not exceed to any perceptible degree than those with two-man operation." The one-man car very often enabled the company to give street car service in thinly populated districts.

The D&I owned six motor cars and two trailers. As wages began to climb with other operating costs, the company began to consider other economies. The ends of the Whedbee Street and the College Avenue line were connected, thus forming a loop. It was possible to eliminate one car and improve service at the same time. The Whedbee Street line was extended south from Elizabeth Street to Edwards Street, west on Edwards to Remington Street, where it joined the old line.

The big snow of 1913 encircles a trolley stranded on the corner of Pitkin and Remington Streets. (Below) Street car activity at College and Mountain during the heyday of the Denver & Interurban. — Both E. S. Peyton Collection

73

The conversion to one-man operation caused some dissatisfaction with the public. The company had hinted without actually promising that new cars would be used when one-man operation became a reality. At this time the track was removed from Edwards Street north to Elizabeth Street, and west one block on Elizabeth to College Avenue, being replaced by the new loop.

Safety was the watchword on the D&I. Crewmen were instructed that the greatest danger to the company and their job was that of accidents and resulting law suits. The only serious accident on record was a collision between Car No. 104 and a steam shovel at the sugar factory in which William Vanderwark was seriously injured. The street car was so badly damaged that it was junked. Trucks, controllers and mechanical parts were used to convert trailer No. 107 to a motor car. The accident happened when Vanderwark heard a passenger shout a warning and thinking he had forgotten to pick up a passenger, looked to the rear of the car. The collision followed immediately. Vanderwark was seriously injured, and not expected to live. He rallied, and served many more years with both the D&I and the Fort Collins Municipal Railway.

Probably the main factor in the downfall of the Denver & Interurban was the seizure and operation of the Colorado & Southern by the United States Railroad Administration in 1917. Since the federal government was interested only in essential transportation units, the D&I was not taken over.

It was left to its own fate as a small and comparatively unimportant company.

The interurban line from Denver to Boulder was separated physically from the Fort Collins city lines, a situation not conducive to efficient management. Wages were high and labor was scarce. Operating expenses were up and some items were impossible to get which were necessary to the proper operation of a street railway. The company was not on a profitable basis, especially the Fort Collins line. There were no surplus funds to meet soaring expenses. The old five cent fare was still in effect. Public sentiment was not too favorable and

All that remained of M-104 after the collision with a steam shovel. — J. O. BEELER (Below) A trolley rolls past the Elk's Hall on Linden Street on a quiet Sunday afternoon. — DENVER PUBLIC LIBRARY WESTERN COLLECTION

complaints began to roll in. Many trolley riders became prosperous enough during the war to be able to own one of those new-fangled automobiles.

Finally in 1918 the D&I was unable to pay interest on its bonds. The company was immediately thrown into receivership by the Guaranty Trust Company of New York City representing the bondholders. W. H. Edmunds, general manager was appointed receiver and there was some talk of abandoning the entire system, including the Denver to Boulder interurban line. Edmunds was a very quiet, unassuming man, but a highly efficient manager. The receivership was soon terminated.

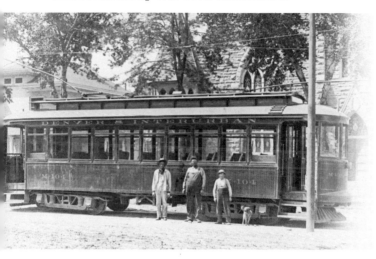

Rover and a young trolley enthusiast stand beside the car barn workers at Howes and Mountain Avenue. — J. O. BEELER COLLECTION

A White Motor Railcar enroute to Nevada for a trial run on the famed Virginia & Truckee pauses for a 30-day run on the Fort Collins line. Although unique, the gasoline street car was not popular with the riding public. — WHITE MOTOR COMPANY

Attempts were made in court to have the D&I declared a part of the Colorado & Southern, making the parent company responsible for the obligations of the city line. The courts ruled that the C&S was completely separate from the D&I, and no longer responsible for the financial problems of the struggling company and the D&I was left to its own resources.

Abandonment was not immediate, but business was rapidly declining. Owners of Lindenmeier Lake claimed that their business had been ruined by poor service. Edmunds asked permission to junk the entire system, pleading war necessity.

On the night of July 10, 1918, without warning, employees were told not to report for work the next day as service was being annuled. Fort Collins awoke the following morning without any form of public transportation. Attempts were made by a private party to operate a bus line, using a 16-passenger Stanley Steamer bus and charging a ten-cent fare. This was of short duration. The city officials began to study the possibility of local operation. In the meantime the White Motor Company proposed operating a gasoline car and equipped an open sightseeing bus with flanged steel wheels for rail operation. This car was put on a 30-day trial service. Gasoline cars had been tried in other parts of the country, but had met with little success. This gasoline street car was not popular. It was rough riding, noisy and smoky. Frequent derailments damaged the steel wheels, causing excessive maintenance. The White Motor Company pointed out that this car was built for trial purposes only, and that they could build an adequate car. The gasoline car was discontinued and again Fort Collins was without service.

Suggestions were made that the city buy and operate the street car lines. Proposals and counter-proposals were made. In the meantime as one newspaper said: "Fort Collins will continue to hoof it."

Today, with a car in every garage, it is difficult to realize the extent to which people of a small city could become dependent upon a street car line. Buses had not yet reached the point where they were dependable, and the automobile of that time was expensive and temperamental. Real estate values in outlying areas were effected, and business at some of the downtown stores sagged.

At long last Edmunds agreed to accept $75,000 for the physical plant. This was some $20,000 less than junk value. It was agreed that the company would be turned over to anyone paying a $5,000 deposit, and that service could be resumed. J. O. Beeler stated that, "cars and track of the D&I were well-maintained and were in fairly good condition, considering the fact that the company had

been losing money for some years." However, the D&I cars were heavy and consumed a high quantity of electric power. To make matters worse, the nearby community of Greeley, Colorado, had just received a new shipment of one-man street cars to revamp their local lines. The citizens of Fort Collins were envious of their neighbor city. Civic and community groups got together and put pressure on city officials to do something.

According to local newspapers, it was claimed that it would cost more than the old cars were worth to restore them to proper running order. The track and overhead required complete rebuilding. It was recommended that: "Cars on hand be disposed of as soon as possible," and that new lightweight cars and lighter power equipment be installed.

An estimate of operating costs was published:

Maintenance of way & structures	$ 4,500
Maintenance of equipment	2,500
Power	6,000
Motormen at $.29 per hour	6,520
Supervision	2,500
TOTAL	$21,750

The Lindenmeier Lake line was to be abandoned and sold. It was estimated that new equipment and faster schedules should increase revenue by about one-third. The following editorial appeared in the *Fort Collins Express*:

BUY THE STREET CAR SYSTEM

"If the city can buy the street car system for a reasonable sum and can operate it at no great annual deficit, it would be a good business proposition to close the deal and take the system over. Fort Collins needs a rapid transit system of some kind. There can be no doubt about that, and it would seem a good business proposition to accept the receiver's offer to sell the system for $75,000. The original cost of the Fort Collins Street Car System was about $315,000, and it is worth today many thousand more as junk than the receiver asked for it. The city will therefore lose nothing on the deal, but on the other hand, stands to reap a good profit on the transaction.".

On January 7, 1919, an election was held. There was little opposition either to the purchase of the new system or the bond issue of $100,000 to pay

The Birney Safety Car came along just in time to salvage many street railway lines. Charles Birney, an engineer for Stone & Webster, developed the new trolley design in 1916. The little car was light in weight, had a single truck, and equipped with safety devices to permit its operation by one man. This feature alone helped cut operating expenses on most systems. The public liked the little cars, however poked fun at them as they bobbed down a street. On the left, one of the dinky cars on Mountain Avenue inbound to the downtown region. — DONALD DUKE (Right) Heart of the one-man car. The operator of a Birney was more like a one-armed paper hanger. Besides running the trolley, he made change, punched transfers and sold monthly passes. DUKE-MIDDLETON COLLECTION (Below) Birney No. 21 glides through City Park on its return to town. — BARNEY NEUBURGER

for it. Publicity was freely given by the newspapers. Typical headlines:

"NOW OR NEVER FOR THE STREET CARS!"

"YOU MUST SAY TODAY WHAT YOU WANT"

"EITHER A CITY OR AN OLD FASHIONED TOWN"

"LOSS OF STREET CAR SYSTEM WILL CRIPPLE CITY FOREVER"

The election carried eight to one for the purchase of the lines and five to one for the bond issue necessary to foot the bill. All of the bonds were sold locally, and one of the papers stated that $500,000 worth could have been sold just as easily.

It was announced that service would not be resumed with the old equipment and before delivery of the new cars, track work would be necessary. An editorial said:

"We are proud of Fort Collins, proud that it is composed of people who not only went over the top in every patriotic war issue, but on a progressive peace issue also responded in a whole-souled manner."

It was stated that four new street cars had been ordered for the municipal system and each car would cost approximately $6,000. Delivery was promised in 40 to 60 days from the time the order reached the factory. The new cars were of the one-man Birney type, named after its designer, C. O. Birney who was employed by the Stone & Webster syndicate. Prior to Birney's revolutionary design, street cars were built to suit an individual system. Birney felt that street cars should be designed to meet the average needs of traction companies and produced on a semi-mass production basis. The result was the Birney Standard Safety Car. The first of these was built by the American Car Company of St. Louis, Missouri. They were single truck, double-end, light weight steel construction, and equipped with full safety equipment (dead-man control which was a button on the controller which would automatically stop the car in case the motorman died or was stricken).

The Western Light & Power Company was awarded the contract to supply power for the line and the overhead line was put in good condition. Track and structures were checked, and where

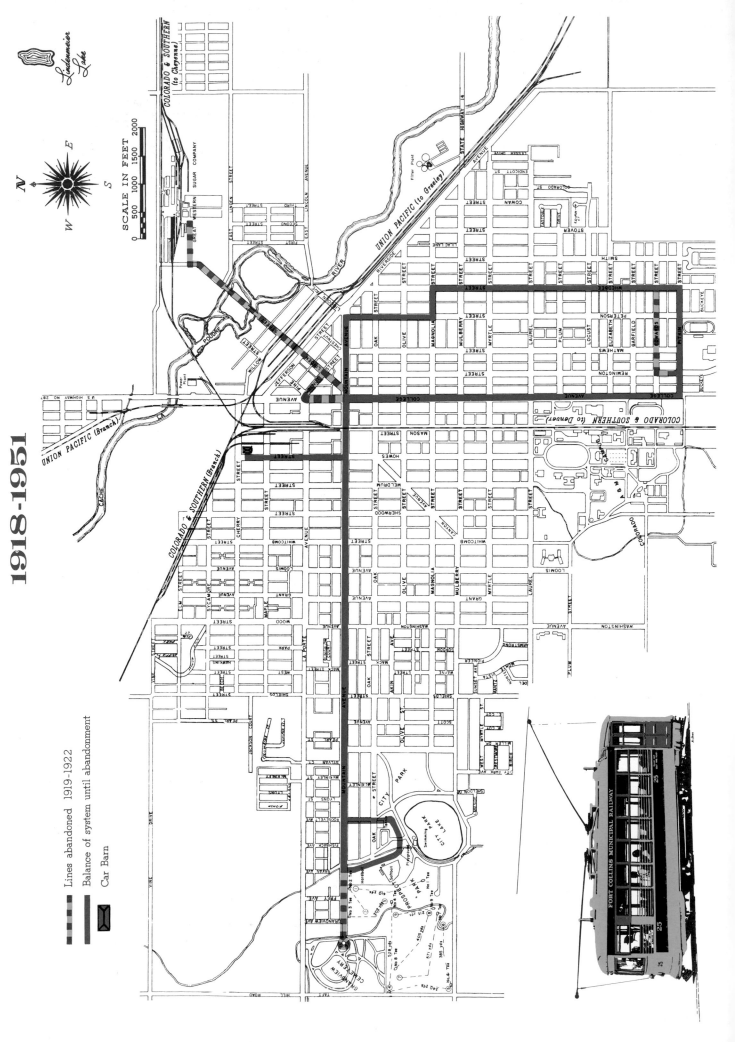

Fort Collins Municipal Railway

1918-1951

Lindenmeier Lake

SCALE IN FEET

0 500 1000 1500 2000

▪▪▪▪ Lines abandoned 1919-1922

▬▬▬ Balance of system until abandonment

◆ Car Barn

FORT COLLINS MUNICIPAL RAILWAY

necessary rails were replaced. The whole system was put in first class condition awaiting the new trolleys.

On May 2, 1919, word was received the cars had been shipped from St. Louis and were in transit. By May 24, the cars arrived on several flat cars and preparations were made for the unloading. A trial run of Car No. 21 was made to establish a schedule. It had been planned to run on a 15-minute headway, but the trials showed that "although the motorman put on some extra speed, the trip took between 17 and 18 minutes." As a result, the old 20-minute schedule was resumed. (Incidently, Car No. 21 which made the trial run was the last car to run on the streets of Fort Collins, the occasion being its removal to the Pioneer Museum in 1953 when it was towed through the streets by a truck.)

Richard S. Baker, assistant city manager of Fort Collins, in an article published in 1950, while the system was still in operation, presented in detail the story of the modernization of the old D&I and the creation of the Fort Collins Municipal Railway. He says:

"Early in 1919 at an election the citizens voted 940 to 132 in favor of buying the system. At the same time a $100,000 bond issue was approved. About the 24th of May, 1919, four Birney Standard Safety Cars were unloaded and put in service. These cars were numbered 20, 21, 22, and 23. In June the city began to dismantle the track and overhead between Andersonville and Lindenmeier Lake, a distance of one mile, about 1,000 feet of steel and wire were taken to Roosevelt Street and used in construction of the City Park Spur. In December 1919, two 75 kw., 600 volt, 125 amp., 1,160 r.p.m. motor generator sets were installed in the carbarns to replace the 500 kw., 550 volt, 750 r.p.m. rotary converter. The generator sets made a saving of about 33⅓ per cent in power. On Labor Day, 1920, a new car was put in service that had been purchased from the National Car Company at a cost of $6,500 plus freight. This was No. 24."

The annual report of the city engineer made available through the courtesy of Baker gives a good picture of the situation shortly after modernization.

"On February 12, 1920, work on the track on South College Avenue was taken up and completed about March 22. On April 13, 1920, dismantling track and overhead from Anderson Corner and the sugar factory was begun, using about 900 feet of material for a spur to the sugar factory time office, on the east side

Car No. 22 gallops along the parkish like center section of Mountain Avenue. — DONALD DUKE

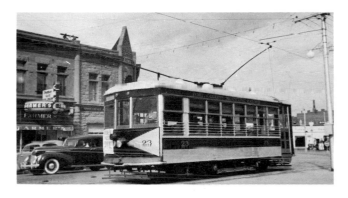

Painted in green and buff livery of the 1940's, No. 23 pauses at the intersection of Mountain and College for a single passenger. — GORDON LLOYD (Below) Fort Collins was famous for its wide streets, and the lawned center parkways provided a perfect right-of-way for the trolleys. Next stop—Colorado A & M College. — BARNEY NEUBURGER

Focal point of downtown Fort Collins was the three-way intersection of Mountain Avenue, College Avenue and Linden Street. Here three trolley cars would meet each other every trip. In the scene above, two cars approach a wye in the center of the street. A third car off to the left is out of range of the camera. On a given signal, all three cars would pass simultaneously on the wye. — DENVER PUBLIC LIBRARY WESTERN COLLECTION *(Right)* Illustration of the three-way meet at street level, truly a sight to behold. This was the most unusual trolley operation in the United States. — BARNEY NEUBURGER

of the Colorado & Southern main line, and the balance hauled up to the barns and stored with other material. By making this change we did away with two railroad crossings that were badly worn and would have to be renewed and maintained at a cost greater than moving the track.

"On May 1, 1920, work was begun on rebuilding and ballasting track on Mountain Avenue from Howes Street to Shields Street, putting in crushed rock ballast and a four inch drain tile at each intersection. This work was completed about August 15.

"The system has more than proved its need to the public. It has held up the standards of our city far above that of a country village and in addition has offered continuous service to its patrons. The utility has operated during periods when other railroads were snowbound. It has paid all operating and maintenance costs

and for a new car since the beginning of the system. Service to the public by the street railway was greatly improved in December 1922, by providing a new ten-minute schedule which seems to be working satisfactorily."

The ten-minute schedule first attempted in 1922 was not satisfactory. Several schedule changes were made and the ten-minute service was discontinued at various times. Finally a new plan was tried out in 1925. Two cars were purchased from the Cheyenne, Wyoming, street railway system, and the following notice appeared in the *Express Courier*, May 4, 1925:

(Monday) "Two way service on the College Avenue and the Whedbee Street line will be inaugurated sometime Tuesday or Wednesday. Regular cars leave the junction (College and Mountain Ave.) at five, 25, and 45 minutes past the hour from 6:25 A.M. to 11:05 P.M. except on Saturdays when cars run until 12:05

A.M. In addition to regular service, split-shift cars will operate on Mountain Avenue and College Avenue lines only, leaving the junction at 15, 35, and 55 minutes past the hour during the busy periods of the day, making the downtown loop in reverse direction.

Ten minute service 6:25 to 8:55 A.M.
Twenty minute service 8:55 to 11:55 A.M.
Ten minute service 11:55 A.M. to 7:35 P.M.
Twenty minute service 7:35 P.M. on."

Even this service did not work out too well, increased revenue not being sufficient to cover additional expenses. During the year 1924, for example, the report of the city commissioners showed that:

"City cars carried 478,848 passengers during 1924. The greatest number in one month, December — 56,674. Lowest number of passengers, April — 35,352.

RECEIPTS

Advertising	$ 1,006.25
Fares	6,452.85
Tickets	17,604.09
Operating maintenance	625.84
TOTAL	$25,689.03

EXPENSES

Operating labor	$13,337.60
Maintenance labor	4,166.86
Operating materials	5,714.79
Maintenance materials	5,024.54
Rebates	46.53
Improvements	1,819.13
TOTAL	$30,109.18"

This would indicate a deficit of $4,420.15. However, in defense of this the commissioners reminded the public that two cars had been purchased from the Cheyenne line. The two Cheyenne cars were shown on the roster of the Fort Collins Municipal Railway as Nos. 25 and 26.

The Fort Collins Municipal Railway remained without any significant change for over 25 years. Service was equal to that anywhere and superior to that found in many larger cities. Cars were clean, well maintained even down to the changing paint schemes. The city of Fort Collins was unique, being the smallest city in the United States having an electric municipal railway system.

During the disintegration of the Denver Tramway, Greeley Electric Railway, Colorado Springs & Interurban Railway, many comparisons were made with the fine operation of the Fort Collins system. In all of these cases, the Greeley line came out decidedly second best and it was not too long before the company abandoned. As was often the case with small properties having inadequate shop equipment and limited financial resources, maintenance was neglected. Cars were unpainted, and

Strolling through the park one day, I ran into car No. 22 lumbering along under the shadows of some big poplar trees. — AL ROSE

Every once in a while an obstinate motor vehicle contested the venerable old trolley for the right-of-way.

operating speed was reduced because the track was in poor shape. Before long the public found another way to travel. The limited amount of nickels dropped in the fare register hardly covered wages, power bills and taxes. That is, when they were paid!

Fort Collins had new cars, track and overhead were in good condition, service was every ten minutes, and further improvements were planned. There were a few accidents of course, none serious, partly because of the modest operating speeds. In 1925 one could not find a more modern street railway operating in the United States than the Fort Collins Municipal Railway. The population of Fort Collins increased in ten years from 8,000 to nearly 20,000 and without a further extension of the street railway. All was not roses, for the family automobile became increasingly popular as a means of travel within town. Street car patronage declined throughout Colorado, while costs rose without an increase in fare.

Traction companies throughout the United States began to consolidate, or cut service. Still the citizens of Fort Collins remained strongly pro-trolley. At four different times, elections were held to determine the fate of the street cars. In each case the voters decided in favor of the trolleys. As a matter of fact the street cars were never legally voted out of Fort Collins. Why would a town hang on to its own street car system? There were several reasons, but the prime point was many feared, and rightly so, that a privately-owned bus line might not last, leaving the city without any public transportation. Besides, the city received much local and national publicity because of its city-owned trolley operation.

The *Saturday Evening Post* published in 1947 an article entitled, "Some of My Best Friends Are Street Cars." If we may quote directly, "For truly fancy performance in the field of transit, no place on earth can beat Fort Collins, Colorado." The article goes on to describe in detail operations of the system, noting that three cars operate on two loops and a long connecting line running in two directions. At no time do cars pass on sidings although there are two passing tracks on the line. Switching operations being carried out on a wye and a spur. At one point three cars pass simultaneously on a wye, located at the corner of Mountain and College Avenue, "truly a sight to behold". In concluding, the following statement is made: "The municipally-owned Fort Collins system holds two impressive records. It has the lowest trolley fares in the nation, five cents a ride, six tokens for a quarter, and a dollar for an unlimited monthly pass — and it makes money." (True at the time the article was written.)

The U. S. highway between Denver-Cheyenne used College Avenue as the main route through Fort Collins. Tourists often pulled their cars to the side of the road to watch one of the dinkies gallop along the line. In the scene above, No. 25 leaves the picturesque center parkway as it nears the downtown region. — AL ROSE *(Below)* A trolley running south on College Avenue worked against the flow of automobile traffic. — BARNEY NEUBURGER

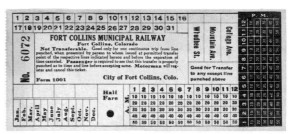

The Fort Collins Municipal Railway had the lowest fare structure in the nation. Five cents for a single ride with transfer, six tokens for a quarter or a dollar for an unlimited monthly pass. Samples of the transfer and pass are shown above. — DONALD DUKE COLLECTION *(Below)* Birney No. 25 on the storage track at the car barn. Cars were painted silver and black with red trim around the windows and door during the last years of operation. — DONALD DUKE

At the Colorado & Southern freight station, one of the Virginia Transit Authority cars arrives aboard a flat car. — E. S. PEYTON

It became impossible to get repair parts for the ancient Birney cars. Many parts had to be made by hand in local machine shops. In an effort to relieve the situation, the city bought two more Birneys at scrap prices plus freight from the Virginia Transit Authority at Norfolk, Virginia. One was to be dismantled to provide spare parts. Upon arrival both cars were in such bad condition that it seemed their purchase had been a mistake. After rebuilding, the new second-hand cars were given Nos. 24 and 25. The author remembers riding both cars at various times. No. 25 remained in service for some time, however No. 24 was removed from service shortly after purchase and used for parts to keep the others running.

Former conductor-motorman Beeler stated that, "The Birneys were well kept and in good condition. They were in much better condition than most people supposed." A large number of new ties were placed in the track during the last few years of operation but were not properly tamped. This caused the track to settle in places, resulting in low joints with high centers. This gave the passengers a peculiar sensation as the trolley glided down the track. The big problem was the track was not properly built from the start. It is common railroad practice to stagger the rail joints thus giving a more even ride. The Denver & Interurban placed the rail joints directly across from each other when the line was built. There is no reason obtainable as to why this. was done, as this practice was not carried out on any of their other operations.

By the late 1940's, the Bussard Bus Company of Englewood, Colorado, was granted a franchise to serve outlying parts of the city. In some cases Bussard offered direct competition to the city-owned trolley lines. Early in 1951, the Birneys began to fall apart one by one. They were replaced as they became unfit for service by a bus. Transfers were honored between the two systems. At last, when only one car was in operating condition the city council decided to substitute buses entirely on a six months trial period. The physical plant was to remain intact until the end of the experiment.

The Norfolk cars were seldom used and only when another car was out of service for repairs. At the upper left, car No. 24 hesitates at the City Park picnic grounds. — AL ROSE (Left) A side view of car No. 24 showing clearly the single truck of the Birney type street car. — DONALD DUKE

Car No. 22 clattered through the streets of Fort Collins for the last time June 30, 1951. This was also the last Birney to operate on the North American continent. — DONALD DUKE *(Below)* February 24, 1953 was a memorable day for Fort Collins. The truck used in pulling the time-honored trolley to the Pioneer Museum got stuck at the crossing of College and Mountain Avenues. The tractor which pulled the car from the barn came to the rescue. — DENVER PUBLIC LIBRARY WESTERN COLLECTION

On June 30, 1951, Car No. 22 clattered through the streets of Fort Collins for the last time, closing the curtain on a colorful past performance. This was to be the last scheduled Birney car operation in the North American continent, and the last street car to operate commercially in the state of Colorado. It was a black day for the citizens of Fort Collins and the electric railway enthusiasts.

During 1953, No. 21 was given to the Pioneer Museum of Fort Collins. With the overhead power turned-off, the old car was pulled from the carbarn by a tractor and then towed disgracefully to the museum site by a truck. It was later placed on a short section of track alongside the museum. The bowed little trolley resting on its pedestal can be viewed by all future generations who will one day ask: "What is a trolley car?"

It would be interesting to gaze into the crystal ball and speculate on a few things. What would have happened if the city of Fort Collins had authorized a small amount of money and leveled up the track, extended the lines to the newly developed areas of the city, and purchased three or four of the streamline PCC type streetcars which could have been secured at scrap prices? Even today many of the old timers wish they had their little old dinkey cars back. ❖❖❖

This beautiful engraving illustrates the first run of Baltimore & Ohio's new electric locomotive
as it rumbles through the dimness of Howard Street Tunnel.—DONALD DUKE COLLECTION

America's First Main Line Electrification

by Donald Duke

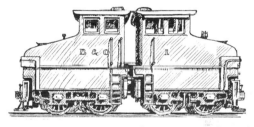

*T*HE word Baltimore carries pioneer meaning to every branch of American transportation. In ocean service, the record of the clipper Baltimore was a tradition of our maritime supremacy. In a similar way the Baltimore & Ohio was our pioneer common carrier steam railroad. The electrification of the B&O's Baltimore Railway Tunnel in 1895 was the first application of electric power to a portion of a main line railroad – another pioneer first.

At the turn of the century, the electrification of portions of steam railroads of the United States was in progress. It was thought that this new means of locomotion might eventually replace the steam locomotive. The publication Steam Locomotive Engineering for September 1895 thought otherwise and had

BALTIMORE BELT RAILROAD.

this to say. "There are hundreds of thousands of every day people who think that electricity is taking the place of steam, and that soon locomotives and stationary engines will be cold in death, fuel useless, and a motor doing all the work. A little inquiry soon will show that the electric current is only a convenient means of conveying power — a belt — and that power can be best and most economically developed by the steam engine. We say, steam is here to stay." Of course these fine gentlemen were prejudiced, yet electrification of steam railroads never did reach its zenith.

In many localities, due to topographical conditions, the maximum amount of service obtainable from steam locomotives had been reached; the electrification of such portions resulted in not only relieving congestion of traffic, but provided the extra capacity to move increased tonnage over the same tracks.

The Baltimore & Ohio Railroad was the first major railroad in the United States to apply electric power to a steam railroad. Ways of improving its facilities for running trains through the city of Baltimore was of prime importance as early as 1886. It became increasingly difficult for the B&O to compete with the growing Pennsylvania Railroad, which had built an all-rail route through the city in 1872. This was accomplished by means of a long tunnel and deep cuts which later were roofed over. Trains on the B&O going north to Philadelphia were required to take a ferry across the Patapsco River from Locust Point to Canton, a distance of three-fourths of a mile. This was not the only bottleneck. B&O trains through South Baltimore were required to crawl through freight yards and run along public streets for several miles. Such time consuming delays were disastrous for the Baltimore & Ohio which was trying to compete in passenger and freight traffic.

In the fall of 1887, it was rumored by Baltimore papers that a new B&O connecting railroad tunnel was to be built under the entire length of Howard Street, similar to the tunnels of the Pennsylvania Railroad. Baltimore citizens received the Howard Street Tunnel plan with keen interest, but not without criticism. Irate citizens wrote letters to the newspapers reminding the town and civic officials what an upset its downtown section had been when Union Station was built. There was the usual nervousness displayed by others concerning the construction hazards of any tunnel which might cause their homes or buildings to fall into on open abyss. Others began letter campaigns to inform the citizenry of the presence of gas and smoke at the Pennsylvania's tunnels, an argument against any tunnel the B&O might wish to construct.

Previously the B & O seriously contemplated building an overhead elevated railroad across town between Camden Station and the Philadelphia stem near Canton. Such a line, mounted on steel structures was patterned after the successful elevated railway of New York and Brooklyn. The line was to run on a private right-of-way free of grade crossings. Immediately the women of Baltimore were on the defensive and condemned the program. Their lovely city upon seven hills to be surrounded by overhead trains and portions never to see the light of day ? Never, not in Baltimore. Business and real estate people feared the lowering of property values which would eventually wreck the town. The elevated plan was deadlocked in court and died aborning.

Topographically the city of Baltimore rises in altitude as one goes north from Camden Station. Whether an elevated or tunnel was the answer to B&O's problem, the railroad was faced with a relatively stiff grade (somewhat less than one percent) the whole distance north, beginning from a dead stop at Camden Station to the cutoff with the main stem near Canton. A grade of such magnitude meant real smoke problems in the proposed tunnel with related danger to both the crews and passengers.

It appeared the B&O had reached the end of the line in its own home city. Management and city officials worked for months in an attempt to readjust the tunnel program to meet all demands. For two years, talks, surveys, plans and programs were set forth, then to be rejected by the city fathers. When the B&O announced that it would use electric power for the haulage of trains through the proposed tunnel, newspapers placed a new importance on the project. Electric locomotives emitted no smoke or fumes, and created little noise. Electric power for trains was something unheard of and when it was established that the General Electric Company was to assist in this project, the newspapers gave the project additional praise. At long last common sense prevailed and the plan was given city approval.

Up to this time, electricity was barely in general use on street railways, let alone to any extent on a main line railroad and in a tunnel. Great tunnels, both in the United States and Europe, still clung to the steam locomotive, its vapors filling the Hoosac and the long bore under Manhattan. The trolley car had come of age, why not electric locomotives to pull regular trains ? The Baltimore & Ohio was soon to show the world it could solve the disagreeable tunnel problem and maybe the future of railroad locomotion.

So was born the Baltimore Belt Railroad. On December 17, 1888, the company was chartered to "construct a railway in the city of Baltimore from Camden Station of the Baltimore & Ohio Railroad, to a connection with the Philadelphia extension of the Baltimore & Ohio Railroad." The enterprise was planned by the officers of the B&O, and the narrow gauge Maryland Central Railroad, thus giving the B&O a means of reaching the heart of the city with its passenger and freight traffic, and the Maryland Central a way of reaching a tidewater terminal.

The work of constructing the tunnels was carried on by the Maryland Construction Company, a separate organization formed by the officers of the two railroads, in which several Baltimore capitalists were represented. By September 4, 1890, construction contracts were let by the Belt Line for construction of the tunnel project. The Belt Line was to be seven and three-fourths miles in length, and the cost of its building and equipment estimated at $6,000,000. The Howard Street Tunnel was to be about 8,350 feet in length, and its cost estimated at $1,750,000, with the land costing an additional $1,000,000. Funds for the enterprise were provided by the issuance of bonds amounting to $6,000,000, bearing five per cent interest. The actual work of construction was begun September 1, 1891, and the laying of tracks was to be completed early in 1895. By the time construction had begun, the Maryland Central gave up the dream of a tidewater terminal and withdrew from the Belt Line Railroad.

The tunnel was one of the longest soft earth tunnels ever driven in the United States. It was to run through the center of the city, immediately under Howard Street, one of Baltimore's principal thoroughfares. It was to be built with almost no interruption to the incessant street car and wagon traffic on the surface, and to secure this result several shafts to the tunnel below were sunk through the cellars of houses and business buildings. The soil through which the tunnel was driven consisted chiefly of sand through which ran seams of gravel, quicksand, and hard species of clay. At times considerable blasting had to be done. Water was of course encountered and to facilitate work, the ground was drained in advance of the heading by means of wells sunk at various points along the route of the tunnel. The only severe cave-in occured in the vicinity of the Baltimore City College, which was ruined. A new college was built by the contractors on the site of the collapsed building. When completed, the final length of the tunnel measured 7,339 feet with a maximum dimension after the cement lining of 27 feet in width and 22 feet in height.

The *Philadelphia Press* of January 3, 1895 reported the following, "The Baltimore & Ohio Railroad is preparing a gigantic coup that will draw Washington and New York nearer together by forty minutes. This is the new $8,000,000 tunnel under the city of Baltimore, by which the transportation of cars across the river at Baltimore will be obviated. There has been a good deal of secrecy maintained by this tunnel, the Baltimore & Ohio people having determined on a great stroke when it is opened. Nobody is allowed to write it up, and all inquiries are met with polite evasions, which tell nothing except that they are building a tunnel which will some time or other be finished. It is, however, declared by the *Boston Transcript* that it is considerably nearer completion than the officials let on — and it is certain that four hours and twenty minutes will take a train through from Washington to New York." The B&O was quite secret about the building of the tunnel in news papers and trade journals. It was not until the bore was officially opened that much in the way of historical reference can be found. Apparently B&O men did not want the rival Pennsylvania Railroad to learn their secrets and this is not a far gone conclusion during this period of railroading. The various railroad companies had a network of spies which would rival today's C.I.A. and put it to shame.

The electrification of the tunnel and the successful operation of trains by electric power offered a great opportunity for the builder. Status in the electrical and transportation world would be in the offing for the one completing the project. General Electric made overtures for the construction of the electric locomotives, effect a system of tunnel lighting and ventilation, electrify the tube for train service and guarantee an engine speed at passenger and freight levels. General Electric won the contract.

Cable traction was suggested by General Electric as the best means of operating electric locomotives through the tunnels. Such a plan was later rejected as inadequate and an overhead means of collection was designed. An old General Electric bulletin stated, "These new locomotives will have sufficient capacity so as to haul the heaviest passenger and freight trains. They will operate from about 1,800 feet in the open of the north portal of the tunnel, through it, and for 4,600 feet beyond the south entrance, or a total distance of 14,500 feet. It is considered that the locomotives will join the rear of each train at the south entrance and push its cars and steam locomotive through to the other end, from which point the steam locomotive will do all the hauling."

In the tunnel itself, the grade was all in one direction, rising on a steady 0.80 per cent ascent all the way. This long grade, while necessitating a pretty steady pull in one direction, was compensated for by allowing all southbound trains to coast through from Mount Royal to Camden Station without attaching an electric locomotive.

The plan of pushing passenger trains through the tunnel was abandoned in view of the possible chance that a car or a steam locomotive might leave the rails in front of the heavy electric locomotive pushing at 30 miles per hour. It was estimated that 100 trains per day would use the bore and a derailment might plug the tunnel for more than one day.

Early day photographs of Howard Street Tunnel and electric railway operations are nearly nonexistant today. The illustrations on these and several of the following pages are reproductions from the publisher's file of old railroad journals. (*Left*) The dim radiance from carbon filament electric bulbs illuminate the black darkness of the tube. (*Right*) Train No. 514, a steam powered passenger accommodation, opened the tunnel May 1, 1895. The locomotive holes through the short break in the bore —future site of Mount Royal Station.

When the tunnel was finally completed early in 1895, only one of the electric locomotives was under construction, although two more were under contract. It was decided to wait until the electric engine arrived before officially opening the new tunnel. The public thought otherwise. People were curious and so were members of the press. Pressure forced the B&O to open the tunnel on May 1, 1895, even with a steam locomotive.

Train No. 514, a passenger from Washington to Philadelphia, was the first train to use the new tunnel. It worked up the steep grade through the tunnel and was nearly out of water by the time it reached Bay View Junction. Steam operation of the tunnel did not last long. The first electric locomotive was on its way to Baltimore from General Electric in Schenectady by June 1, 1895.

The first trial run with locomotive No. 1 was made June 27, 1895. The *Baltimore Sun* in its edition of June 28, 1895 remarked, "INFORMAL TEST OF WONDERFUL LOCOMOTIVE—Runs Through Tunnel and Hauls Its Steam Companion Along With Ease — Yesterday, an informal test of this 100-ton machine was made. There is no uncertainty about it now — it pulls. At 11 o'clock yesterday morning the current was turned on and electric locomotive No. 1, the first of the Baltimore & Ohio, and first of the world as well, was pushed from its position on a side track by steam locomotive No. 820 to a cut near Camden Station. The first run to North Avenue was made in seven minutes at a speed of 20 miles per hour."

In just seven minutes the first operating main line electric locomotive to run on American rails became a historical fact. The engine was the wonder of the age. As it rested on a siding on the future site of Mount Royal Station, a great crowd gathered to look over this electrical monster. Many stood quite close to the machine, their mouths open in amazement. To excite the crowd, the motorman began to yank on the whistle cord. Many were frightened and took to the hills, others pushed even closer. This was such a sensation the *Baltimore Sun* went on to say, "Bellowing bullfrogs, croaking foghorns and shrieking steam-whistles would have to form a syndicate to beat the hoot from electric locomotive No. 1. It is as loud as the whistle on an Atlantic steamer. The mightiness of this voice is explained by the fact that there are carried on the locomotive, great reservoirs of compressed air, which are used for the operation of the train air brakes. The air is compressed by a pump driven by electric motors."

Newspapers referred to this strange newcomer to the rails as a "giant". In contrast to the steam locomotive of the day, it was a "giant". Old No. 1 would resemble a mere pygmy if it could be placed beside one of Pennsylvania Railroad's GG-1 electrics of our generation.

The world's first trial run with an electric locomotive was made June 27, 1895. At 11 o'clock that morning, the current was officially turned on. No. 1 was pushed from its position on a side track to the start of the overhead system alongside the powerhouse. Before the memorable event took place, Baltimore & Ohio officials and General Electric engineers posed for the wet-plate camera.

Locomotive Engineering N.Y.

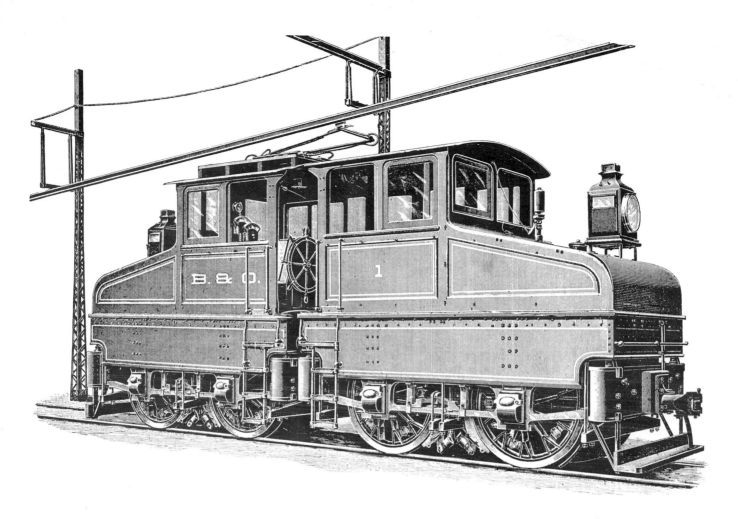

The new electric locomotives were formed in two similar parts, each supported on a truck and coupled together to make one complete unit. The cab located in the center of each section resembled the pilothouse of a ship with the steering wheel operating hand brakes rather than rudder.

The new electric locomotives were the most massive in the history of steam or electric transportation. The weight of each of the three engines was 95-tons placed on eight driving wheels. In this way full tractive power could be developed and this was more than twice the weight on drivers of the heaviest steam locomotive. Each locomotive had two trucks and wheels were 62 inches in diameter. There were four motors, two to each locomotive truck or one per axle. The four motors were gearless, the armature being carried on a sleeve. Spiders were shrunk on the ends of these sleeves, and the drivers were rotated by the spindle-arm which projected between the spoke. For its time, the power trucks were a massive piece of working machinery. Each motor had an output of 360 h.p., or a total of 1,440 for the complete locomotive. These locomotives were provided with sand boxes, automatic air-brakes and train brakes, plus all the controlling equipment necessary for performing the duties of a steam locomotive.

Each locomotive was formed in two similar parts, each supported on a truck and coupled together to form one complete unit of motive power. The cab was placed in the center, one cab in each section affording the motorman a clear view regardless of direction. The balance consisted of sloping ends. Thus was born the heavy duty "steeple" cab locomotive. The cab was constructed of sheet metal with wooden frames, one end carrying a headlight and bell, the other a whistle and headlight.

A test of the first complete truck, representing a half of the locomotive was made at the Schenectady plant of General Electric. In order to obtain the necessary load, a heavy six-wheel steam locomotive was coupled to the electric truck. The machines were then sent in opposite directions, pulling as in a tug-of-war. The electric had a slight advantage over the steamer in weight on the driving wheels, and for this reason pulled the steam engine down the track with apparent ease. It was proved that electric power as a means of locomotion could

Each locomotive had four electric motors, two to each locomotive truck or one per axle. In the view above, a double motor truck. (*Below*) End view of the truck showing one of the motors after the top field frame had been raised.

Technical trade journals classified the new electrics as the "steeple cab" type locomotive because of the steeplelike sloping ends. The electric current carried in the overhead trough at the left was transmitted to the motors by means of a brass shoe mounted on the end of the pantograph like trolley frame.

start a greater load than a steam engine, given the same weight on drivers.

The *Railroad Gazette* carried an extensive article about the Baltimore & Ohio locomotive in its issue of October 4, 1895. It went on to say, "The first of the lot of three electric locomotives to be built by General Electric for the Baltimore & Ohio tunnels at Baltimore is in active service. The second one is being shipped in parts. The contract requires the engines to haul 15 loaded passenger cars and a steam locomotive at 35 mile an hour or 30 loaded freight cars and a locomotive at 15 miles an hour through the tunnel up an 0.8 per cent grade; the object being to keep the tunnel free from locomotive smoke, which would of course be aggravated when pulling up the grade . . . There have been some changes on the electric locomotive since it was put in service, but probably not more than might be expected from the limited experience had so far with such motors. The locomotive is now pulling all the eastbound freight trains through the tunnel, that is about 12 trains a day. The speed made with the guaranteed load is not so fast as agreed upon. About eight miles an hour is all that the locomotive is capable of making with the 30 loaded cars and a locomotive, according to the statement of the engineers on the ground. It is said that the motors will not stand the current required to haul such a train up the grade at 15 miles an hour. This is not to be wondered at when it is known that the current required at eight miles an hour is 1,500 amperes, the motors being in series so that all the current flows through all of the motors . . . The locomotive is not being used now on passenger trains. The smoke clears from the tunnel between trains when pulled by steam locomotives, if the trains are not too close together, so that the freedom from smoke that could be obtained by the use of the electric locomotives is not very important. The steam locomotives on the freight trains that are hauled through make a good deal of smoke while in the tunnel and moving at eight miles an hour . . . Whatever may be the outcome of the use of electric locomotives in the Baltimore tunnel, there is one valuable practical lesson already; there is a possibility of getting any reasonable pull with an electric locomotive. This fact will be impressed on the mind of anyone who sees the machine take hold of a train of 30 cars and start without using the slack. In the matter of speed, there is nothing about this service that is intended to show how fast electric locomotives can be run. Taken as a whole, the Baltimore tunnel engine is a very interesting mechanism, and well worth the trip to Baltimore to see the locomotive pull a train."

The first public operation of the new electric locomotive was made July 1, 1895, when B&O officials hosted a special run for civic dignitaries and the press. The train consisted of No. 1, steam locomotive No. 632 and four polished cars from the famous train *Royal Blue*. The special left Camden Station for a roundtrip to North Avenue through the Howard Street Tunnel. Many stops were made in order to familiarize the guests with the tunnel and the unique electrical system. On the return run, the special paused in the cut just east of Camden Station for the photograph shown above. This view is obviously posed, since the westbound trip was downhill and electric locomotives never used. By 1897 a low level station with train platforms was built near this location. (*Right*) Momento of the first official run showing the original telegraphic train order, views of the train, overhead and tunnel.—BOTH SMITHSONIAN INSTITUTION

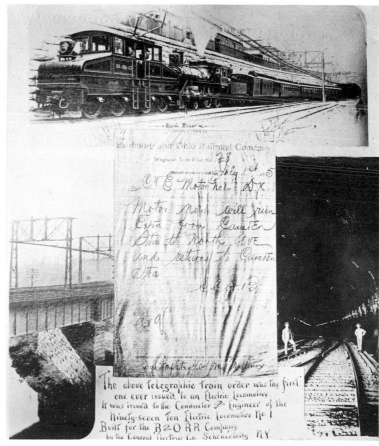

General Electric engineers continued to make improvements to the locomotive. On November 8, 1895, the *Railroad Gazette* stated, "A few days ago a test was made with a dynamometer car placed between the electric locomotive and a train consisting of 22 cars loaded with coal, one caboose and two dead locomotives. The total weight was 1,068 tons. On the grade in the tunnel an average drawbar pull of some 25,000 pounds was obtained from the dynamometer diagram. The speed at this point was 11 miles per hour. Comparisons with the diagrams obtained in similar service with steam locomotives showed a remarkable uniform and steady pull by the electric engine . . . A further test made with another train, consisting of 36 cars, one caboose and three dead engines was made. This was a regular through freight train with a local freight attached, and the total weight was 1,600 tons. It was hauled with ease through the tunnel and calculations from previous dynamometer records and the drawbar pull per ampere showed a drawbar pull of over 45,100 pounds."

The more tonnage added to the consist of a train seemed to have little effect on the pulling power of the electric locomotive. There was not a single train which could hold itself together that was heavy enough to cause the electric to slip its wheels under ordinary fair conditions. The capacity of the locomotive was not reached, but the guaranteed speed was something which puzzled the General Electric engineers. It was shown with a few trial runs with passenger trains that the guaranteed speed of 30 miles per hour could be attained. Actually, speeds of 35 to 40 miles with 500-ton trains were made. An exhibition of high speed was made with the locomotive running at 61 miles per hour for a short time without the slightest trouble with overhead collector or motors.

Steam Locomotive Engineering for October 1895 made this observation about the performance of No. 1. It said, "During a recent visit to Baltimore we found that the large electric locomotive, designed to handle the business in the Baltimore & Ohio tunnels, spends most of the time in the side track undergoing changes. The railroad men around Camden Station do not regard the big motors as much of a success, and there are indications that the cost of pulling trains through the tunnel by electric motors will be much heavier than was anticipated." Such feelings were, of course, pure sour grapes.

On November 29, 1895, the second locomotive arrived in Baltimore in pieces and was immediately assembled. The third locomotive left the General Electric plant during May 1896. When this engine was assembled, complete electrification of the Baltimore Railway Tunnels took place.

In the original installation, electrical energy was supplied to the locomotives through an overhead system of power distribution. The current was car-

The electric current was carried along an inverted trough or channel of metal placed at an angle between the tracks. The scene above was taken at North Avenue.—SMITHSONIAN INSTITUTION

ried along an inverted trough or channel of metal placed at an angle between the tracks. Since the tunnel was low in many places, it was decided that the trough could not be placed directly over the cars, but should be located in the middle of the tunnel between the two tracks. Outside of the tunnel, the trough was still between the parallel tracks, but it was elevated to a height of 22 feet, while inside the tunnel it was 17 feet from top to rail. The trough was supported by a series of transverse supports or bridges, from which chains of iron rod were suspended. In the tunnel, the channel (which was the substitute for the trolley wire) was suspended by insulated supports from the roof. Current was carried to the channel by three copper feed cables, each consisting of 61 wires. The motors of the electric locomotives received the current through a brass shoe. This shoe slid along the channel as the engine moved along the right-of-way. The shoe was connected to a jointed frame or diamond which was similar to today's pantograph. The frame was raised or lowered automatically, adjusting itself to the height of the overhead.

Where there was a track switch, a tongue worked by a lever actuated the switch and at the same time re-directed the shoe of the frame. This unusual system of current collection was the first installation of its kind in the world. It promised to give excellent even contact at all times, and General Electric engineers were pleased.

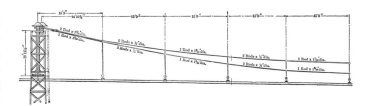

The trough was supported by a series of transverse supports or bridges from which chains or iron rods were suspended. (*Below*) Two types of supports carrying the trough.

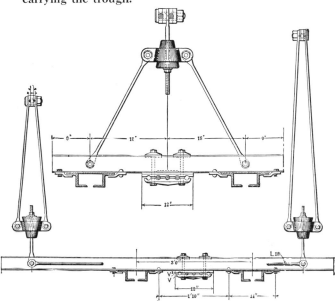

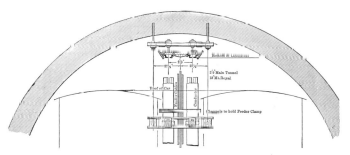

In the tunnel, the channel was suspended by insulated supports from the roof.

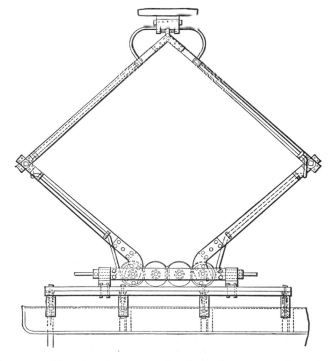

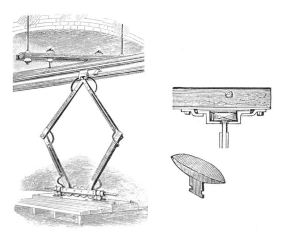

The electric motors received the current through a brass shoe which slid along the channel as the engine moved. The shoe was connected to a jointed frame or diamond mounted atop the locomotive.

As with any new installation which had not been tried by actual performance tests, there were bound to be problems. This overhead system did not prove to be the answer to electric railroad current collection. The presence of gases from the exhaust of steam locomotives as they were pulled through the bore pitted the contacts and many short circuits developed. The constant seepage of ground water from the ceiling of the tunnel, presented the B&O with another real problem. The contact shoes gliding along the channel would become red hot and expand to such an extent that they would become lodged and freeze to a particular spot. This would cause the train to stop dead with a sudden jerk. When this occured the train had to be taken apart in sections with a steam locomotive doing the pulling. The General Electric engineers blamed the heating on imperfect contact due to the presence of moisture within the tunnel. The sealing of the walls and painting of the interior of the tunnel with white paint in several layers helped to alleviate this problem.

With the introduction of the 600-volt ground third-rail system prior to the turn of the century, the B&O immediately adapted this plan and made arrangements for the construction of the third-rail and eventual removel of the overhead. Before this was done the overhead was extended north to Waverly Tower to assist trains on the grade from North Avenue. The line was extended south to Baylies near Camden Station where a carhouse was erected to store and service the new electric power. This extension gave the B&O 3.75 miles of electrified line and included ten tunnels.

Late in 1900 work was begun on the third-rail and by March 1902 the line was completed. The third-rail was laid next to the outside walls of the tunnel for safety reasons. The third-rail consisted of an inverted double "T" type rail supported on cast iron brackets with insulators. It was placed about two feet above the level of the rail. The third rail-shoes were mounted on the locomotive trucks and picked up the power from the top of the rail as the locomotive moved along. The third-rail system was more effective than the overhead and created few power problems from that time on.

At the time the Belt Line and the tunnels were under construction, electric lighting and the use of electric power except for street railways was not common in Baltimore. There was not a single power plant capable of accepting the load of the Belt Line. General Electric erected a power plant for the B&O at Camden Station which supplied current for the railway and other requirements such as station, shops, tunnel lighting. Actually the power house was two separate plants — the generating plant and the lighting plant. Current was generated by five direct connected engines and generators. Each horizontal tandem compound Allis-Corliss machine developed 700 h.p. and was coupled to a 500 Killowatt multipolar generator. The machines compounded 600 volts with no load and 700 volts at full capacity.

By 1909 the increase in traffic brought about a search for public power. The power companies contracted to furnish 13,200 volts at 25 cycles. This was connected to a new B&O rotary converter substation near the Mount Royal Station. In 1914 the old power house at Camden was abandoned and all public power was purchased until electrification was discontinued.

One of the real innovations of the whole operation was the complete electric lighting of the bore. It also was planned to place lighted electric clocks along the tunnel walls, for it was feared that the electric current might disturb the engineer's

The first freight train assisted through the Howard Street Tunnel by an electric locomotive paused for a trackside portrait at the Bolton lot, an area where there was a break in the tunnel of about 557 feet. This space was later roofed over when Mount Royal Station was completed. (*Opposite Page*) General Electric erected a power plant near Camden Station which supplied current for the railway and other requirements such as the station lighting, electric locomotive shops and tunnel lights.

watches. Such fears, of course, proved groundless, but at the time few really knew what electricity might do.

The location of stations along the new Belt Line presented some problems. The Camden Station was an old structure and neither its location nor its fittings were attractive. When the plans for the Belt Line were completed, a new station situated in the residential portion of the city formed a part of the over-all plan. From the very beginning there was general public feeling that the main station of the Belt Line — future main line station of the Baltimore & Ohio in its home city — should be downtown at the intersections of the tunnel and Baltimore Street.

Such a station was never built, although a great deal of time and effort went into the excavation and construction of an underground opening beside the tunnel. The open region would have been filled in by subterranean train platforms similar to New York Central's Grand Central Terminal. Today Baltimore's new civic center which is built over the proposed station has not erased the remains of this abortive underground dream.

The Mount Royal Station was the first of the Belt Line stations. This uptown monument was erected on the Bolton lot, an area where there was a break in the tunnels of about 557 feet. This wide opening was wholly within the finest residential section of Baltimore. Here existed a deep cut with sloping grassy sides, and the ideal situation for a station.

Mount Royal was built with its ground floor on a level with the tracks, thus placing it a considerable distance below the surface of the street. The roof of the main part of the building was about level with the street. The station was constructed of early Renaissance design and built of granite. A striking 150 foot clock tower was placed in the center of the structure and before long it was a Baltimore landmark. The tracks were spanned by a trainshed 400 feet long, separated from the station by a platform. A roof type platform was extended all around the structure more or less enclosing it from the outside elements. Entrance to the grounds was made by an inclined driveway. With green lawn and formal gardens, it is no wonder Edward Hungerford, B&O's famous historian,

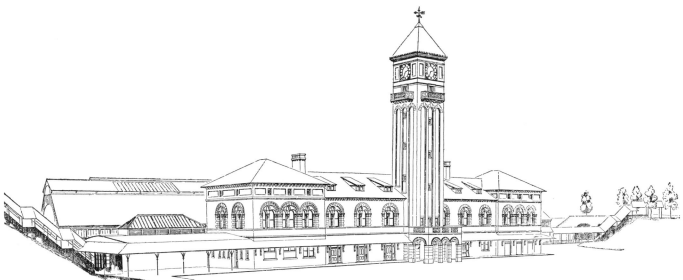

Perspective view of Mount Royal Station prior to construction. (*Below*) Floor plan of the station and the trainshed. The station platform was almost completely roofed over between the tunnel portals.

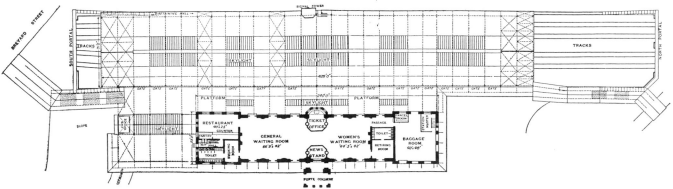

Trackside view of Mount Royal, B&O's uptown station of early Renaissance design. The scene above was taken during the construction of the edifice and looks toward the south portal. When the station opened September 1, 1896, these tracks were spanned by a giant trainshed. (*Right*) General plan of the station site as located in a residential section of Baltimore. The station with its formal gardens and green lawns soon became a landmark.

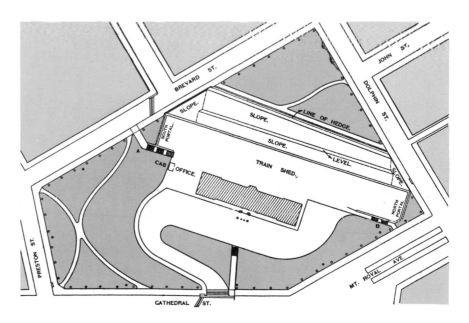

In the waning light of the warm afternoon sun, a "Royal Blue Line" passenger train drawn by electric locomotive No. 1 sweeps into the grand trainshed of Mount Royal Station. This magnificent time exposure reproduced from an original glass plate, captures the nostalgic breath of turn of the century railroading. — SMITHSONIAN INSTITUTION

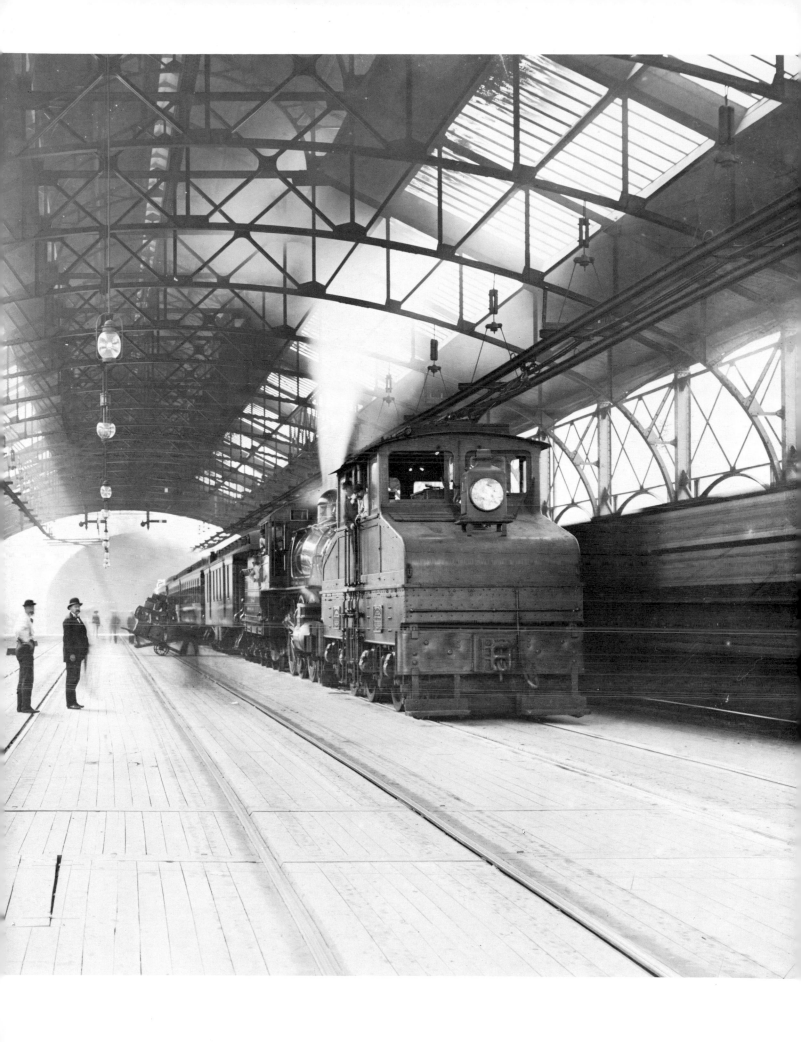

called Mount Royal Station, "One of the most convenient and handsome passenger terminals in the land."

For a time after completion of the tunnel all through trains which traversed the main line backed in and out of old Camden Station, just as they had done in the days of the ferry transfer. In 1897, a low-level station in the cut just below the old station was built, complete with train shed, long platforms. To reach the old station stairs and elevators led directly to the concourse above.

As tonnage increased through the tunnel, four additional locomotives were acquired in 1903. The 75-ton engines were designed exclusively for freight service. Each locomotive was made up of two 75-ton sections, forming a complete locomotive coupled together of 150-tons. This combination provided enough power to move a 1,600-ton freight train including steam locomotive up the steep grade with ease.

The new engines were numbered 5 to 8, and resembled a box on wheels rather than a locomotive. They were far different in appearance from the original three which had a cab in the center with sloping ends. The box-cabs were considered to be more roomy and offered the operator more visibility. In 1906, one more unit of this type was secured from General Electric. Number 9 was a single unit and could be coupled when needed to either set to form a three locomotive unit of 120,-000 pounds tractive power.

With the introduction of steel passenger cars and steel sheathed freight equipment, it was found that the present stable of electric motive power could no longer keep pace with the increasing train weights. The Detroit River Tunnel Company (Michigan Central) had placed several cab units in service during February 1910, and the Baltimore & Ohio electrical engineer went to Detroit to inspect the locomotive performance and power. So impressed was he, that an order was placed immediately for two similar locomotives to be ready for service during November the same year.

The 90-ton locomotives were designed by General Electric, as were all the Belt Line electrics, but the mechanical portion was constructed by the American Locomotive Company. The cab resembled the type popular for switching on interurban railways, yet the trucks and running gear were designed for the demands of trunk line service. Built as No. 11 and 12, the new power weighed 184,000 pounds, had 50-inch wheels, a horsepower rating of 1,000, and a maximum starting effort of 46,000 pounds. The running gear was articulated and consisted of two four-wheel trucks connected through a massive hinge.

Four new 75-ton electric locomotives designed exclusively for slow speed freight service were acquired in 1903. Each locomotive was made up of two sections coupled together to form a 150-ton unit. At the right, the European looking Nos. 5 and 6 as they arrive at the Baltimore shops from General Electric. The locomotives are so new the board over the headlight had not been taken down. (*Below*) The hum of traction motors fill the air as three electrics coupled in multiple roll along with a freight drag on the Belt Line Railway.—BOTH SMITHSONIAN INSTITUTION

One of the two 90-ton locomotives designed by General Electric in 1910 is shown above. The engine resembled the type used on interurban railways, yet this brute was built for heavy main line service. The two four-wheel trucks were connected by a massive hinge which may be seen in this builders photograph.—SMITHSONIAN INSTITUTION (*Below*) Two similar engines Nos. 13 and 14 were added to the roster in 1912 when old Nos. 1, 2 and 3 were retired from service.—COLLECTION OF GERALD M. BEST

At the right, two electrics rumble toward the end of their run. As the freight nears Huntington Avenue Tower, the steam engine begins to take hold of the train. The electrics are then cut off "on the fly" and run ahead, taking a crossover into the clear. The freight behind steam, then continues up the main line at full speed.—SMITHSONIAN INSTITUTION

Two more similar engines were added to the fleet in 1912 when old Nos. 1, 2 and 3 were retired from service. While the old monsters had years of life in them, they could not cope with the increased train weight. Number 1 was retained for the Fair of the Iron Horse, then later scrapped along with the other two engines. In 1923, two more locomotives, Nos. 15 and 16 were added. Although of the same basic design, they had greater power. Tipping the scales at 242,000 pounds, the new power had a tractive effort of 60,500 pounds. Four years later Nos. 17 and 18 were added to the roster.

Mount Clare shops rebuilt Nos. 11 through 14 in 1923, increasing their weight to 240,000 pounds and tractive power to 60,000 pounds. With eight heavy duty electric locomotives, the B&O was able to handle any load placed upon the tunnels. By 1927, the old box-cabs were withdrawn from service and scrapped.

Aside from the tunnel motors, there was still one other electric locomotive running around Baltimore. This little 0-4-0 electric switcher was used to shove cars around Baltimore's waterfront at Fell's Point. The donkey engine used overhead power from the Baltimore Transit Company and a trolley pole collected the current. Old No. 10 was built by General Electric in 1909 and utilized until 1954. The machine is now preserved at the Balti-

more & Ohio Transportation Museum at Baltimore.

When the tunnel first opened, manual block signals were first used, then replaced in 1912 by a line control system. Outside the tunnel automatic color signals protected the right-of-way. By 1920 color light signals were used on the entire Belt Line. Signaling kept pace with modern improvements, and not one accident report can be found which lists an electric locomotive. An amazing record to say the least.

The designers of the tunnel never imagined there would be a day when a box car would not clear the ample arches they provided and for 42 years the clearance within the tunnel was sufficient. However, during this same time period both locomotive and railroad rolling stock grew in size. By 1937 the need for additional clearance above the cars was acute. The tunnel was so constructed that it was too costly to lower the floor and B&O engineers solved this problem by constructing a gauntlet track down the center of the tunnels. When cars of unusual width or height were to be handled the train was run over the gauntlet track which straddled the eastbound and westbound main line.

The gauntlet track solved the first hurdle, but how were the locomotives to obtain their power in the center of the tunnel? The third-rail was located along the base of the tunnel on each side, the distance from the third-rail when using the gauntlet

ELECTRIC LOCOMOTIVES
BALTIMORE & OHIO RAILROAD

NUMBER	CLASS	TYPE	BUILDER	GENERAL ELECTRIC BLDRS NO.	AMERICAN LOCOMOTIVE BLDRS NO.	BUILT	DRIVERS	ENGINE WT.	TRACTIVE EFFORT	HORSEPOWER	REMARKS	NOTE
1	LE-1	0-4-4-0	GE	1413	–	1895	62 in.	196,000#	49,000#	1,440	Retired 1912	A
2	LE-1	0-4-4-0	GE	1414	–	1895	62 in.	196,000#	49,000#	1,440	Retired 1912	
3	LE-1	0-4-4-0	GE	1415	–	1895	62 in.	196,000#	49,000#	1,440	Retired 1912	
5	LE-2	0-4-4-0	GE	1804	–	1903	42 in.	160,000#	40,000#	800	Retired 1927	
6	LE-2	0-4-4-0	GE	1805	–	1903	42 in.	160,000#	40,000#	800	Retired 1934	
7	LE-2	0-4-4-0	GE	1806	–	1903	42 in.	160,000#	40,000#	800	Retired 1934	
8	LE-2	0-4-4-0	GE	1807	–	1903	42 in.	160,000#	40,000#	800	Retired 1934	
9	LE-2	0-4-4-0	GE	2343	–	1906	42 in.	160,000#	40,000#	800	Retired 1934	
10	CE-1	0-4-0	GE	3018	–	7-1909	33 in.	19,400#	4,800#	54	B&O Museum	B
11	OE-1	0-4-4-0	ALCO-GE	3136	46898	3-1910	50 in.	184,000#	46,000#	1,000		B
12	OE-1	0-4-4-0	ALCO-GE	3137	46899	4-1910	50 in.	184,000#	46,000#	1,000		B
13	OE-2	0-4-4-0	ALCO-GE	3804	50583	3-1912	50 in.	200,000#	50,000#	1,100		B
14	OE-2	0-4-4-0	ALCO-GE	3805	50584	3-1912	50 in.	200,000#	50,000#	1,100		B
15	OE-3	0-4-4-0	ALCO-GE	8946	64125	7-1923	50 in.	242,000#	60,500#	1,100	Retired 1952	B
16	OE-3	0-4-4-0	ALCO-GE	8947	64126	7-1923	50 in.	242,000#	60,500#	1,100	Retired 1952	B
17	OE-4	0-4-4-0	ALCO-GE	10341	67225	4-1927	50 in.	240,000#	60,000#	1,100		B
18	OE-4	0-4-4-0	ALCO-GE	10342	67226	4-1927	50 in.	240,000#	60,000#	1,100		B

NOTES:

A – No. 1 was retained for the "Fair of the Iron Horse" the famous centenary pageant held at Halethorpe near Baltimore, September 24 through October 8, 1927. The engine was then scrapped.

B – Between the years 1942 and 1949, locomotives numbered 10 through 18 carried road numbers 150 through 158 respectively. During the later part of 1949 the numbers were changed back to the original 10 through 18 until the electric locomotives were retired.

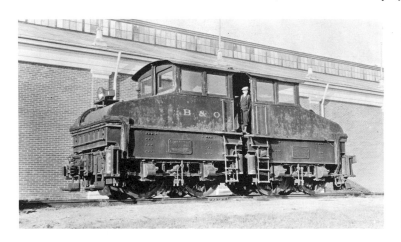

Electric motors Nos. 154 and 153 return to the south portal for another transfer freight. *(Upper left)* Old No. 1 as it appeared shortly after the "Fair of the Iron Horse" held at Baltimore during 1927. *(Left)* The little 0-4-0 electric switcher used to shift cars around Baltimore's waterfront at Fell's Point. — Three Illustrations Collection of Gerald M. Best

THE ELECTRIC LOCOMOTIVES

Silent as night we make our flight
  Through the shadowy Baltimore zone.
With never a sound but the echoing ground
  And our warning bell's clear tone,
We skim and trail along the rail,
  Silent and alone.

By the glow of the stars we race our cars,
  Till Mount Royal lights are near;
The click of the wheels and the purr of steel
  Are the gladdening sound we hear
As we set the pace in our headlong race,
  When the signal lights show clear.

In snow or rain we haul our train,
  Sure of our speed and power,
And the semaphores gleam—but the passengers
    dream
  As we rush past signal bridge and tower,
Till we halt on time to the echoing chime
  When the big clock makes the hour.

⚬⚬⚬⚬⚬

Camden Station shown in the upper left, as it appeared in 1963. This vintage station is a far cry from the stately Mount Royal structure. (*Left*) South end of the tunnel as it looks today. The double track and gauntlet has been removed in favor of a single track down the center so as to accommodate the passage of auto rack cars through the bore. Camden Station and the stub end tracks are to the left of the illustration. — BOTH HERB HARWOOD

track was over four feet. A third-rail closer to the gauntlet track was impossible. At first, an overhead catenary was considered, the idea being abandoned due to the excessive installation cost and overhead wires would limit clearance.

A self-adjusting third-rail shoe mechanism was installed on each locomotive and automatically followed the existing third-rail whether the train was on normal track or on the gauntlet. The shoes were placed on swinging beams located on one side of the locomotive only, as the locomotive was never turned around.

The coming of the diesel age finally killed the tunnel electrification. The basic reason for the change, besides economy, was the elimination of the stops at Camden Station to pick up the electric locomotive, thus blocking street crossings in South Baltimore. The diesel helpers were attached to trains at Mount Winans, south of the congested region, and freight trains had sufficient power already attached to cause them to by-pass the elec-

tric power anyway. Final runs using electric locomotives were made September 1, 1952.

With the final withdrawal of the last New York scheduled passenger train in April 1958, old historical Mount Royal Station served little purpose. From 1958 to 1961 the grand old station contiued to be a terminal for the Baltimore-Washington commuter trains which were largely RDC rail cars. Finally on July 1, 1961 it closed its door to the public and the famous waiting room rocking chairs moved no more.

The Baltimore & Ohio kept title to the structure until its sale to the Maryland Art Institute in 1964. Up to that time the building was boarded up and the four clocks in the tower continued to run. A large illuminated "B&O" electric sign was lighted each night.

Today the old electrics rest on the other side of Jordan, yet on a warm summer's night about old Mount Royal Station there still echoes the hum of the electric motors. ❖❖❖

The Single Drivered Steam
LOCOMOTIVE IN THE WEST

by Gerald M. Best

THE STEAM LOCOMOTIVE with but one pair of driving wheels was a common sight during the first two decades of railroad building and operation in the United States, from 1830 to 1850. Of the first 150 locomotives built by the Baldwin Locomotive Works, the large majority were of the 4-2-0 type, with a four-wheel leading truck and a single pair of drivers. Almost every locomotive builder of that period tried a hand at building single drivered locomotives only to have the 4-4-0, or American type supplant the "singles" in the 1840's. Later locomotives of six and eight driving wheels followed the 4-4-0's, as the demands of traffic required more and more power.

The use of a single pair of drivers was much in favor in Europe in the early days of railroads there; with long stretches of level track with few curves, the Great Western Railway in England retained this type of locomotive for fast express trains well into this century. In the early 1850's there was a short-lived revival of the "single" in the United States, for use on local passenger trains of one or two cars. Among the "singles" built in 1851 was the famous *Pioneer*, built by Seth Wilmarth for the Cumberland Valley Railroad, and now at the Smithsonian Institution in Washington, D. C. Two others were built by the Boston Locomotive Works for the New York & Erie. These were 4-2-2 type with 67-inch drivers, 15x20-inch cylinders and weighing 25 tons. The writer's grandfather, Martin V. Heller, once related that as a baggage boy at the New York & Erie station at Greycourt, New York, in 1852, he and two other teenagers employed around the station used to plague the engineer of the westbound morning accommodation train, which usually consisted of two cars hauled by a locomotive with only a single pair of driving wheels. The boys waited until just the instant the conductor signalled the engineer to start, then hung onto the rear platform railings, digging their heels into the ties, and if the track was wet, the engine's wheels would slip and could not start the train. The engineer usually knew what was happening, and would come roaring back with a large club in his hands, chasing the boys away until the fireman could get the train rolling. Needless to say, with the heavy grades on the New York & Erie's line to Port Jervis, the "singles" lasted only a few years in main line service.

During the Civil War, locomotives were at a premium, and in early 1863 the Danforth & Cooke Locomotive Works of Paterson, New Jersey turned out a few single drivered locomotives to sell either to the U. S. Military Railroad or any line in urgent need of light locomotives for passenger service. They were patterned after a pair of this type which were built for the Cleveland, Painesville & Ashtabula Railroad in 1859. With 54-inch drivers, 11x15-inch cylinders and weighing about 25 tons, the total number of these "singles" built in 1863 is not known, as the shop records of Danforth & Cooke were lost in a fire in 1870. We know that at least seven were built, proof being obtained through photographs and railroad company records. Of these seven, four came to the Pacific Coast in 1863 and 1864, one of them surviving to this day as the famous *C. P. Huntington*, Southern Pacific No. 1.

Purchased by Collis P. Huntington, Vice President of the newly formed Central Pacific Railroad, the engine was named after him. The other "single", of slightly different design, was named after Chief Engineer T. D. Judah. The engine *C. P. Huntington* was loaded aboard the sailing vessel *Success*, and the *T. D. Judah* made the jour-

Lake Shore & Michigan Southern No. 190 built by Danforth & Cooke in 1859 was a prototype of the "C. P. Huntington" and other singles of 1863. For years this locomotive hauled the pay car for which is was admirably suited. — G. M. Best Collection.

Rensselaer & Saratoga No. 25, the "S. M. Craver" was built at the same time as the "C. P. Huntington," but was rebuilt with a longer firebox. — G. M. Best Collection (Right) An 1863 vintage Danforth & Cooke single with a two-wheel truck. Two engines of this design were sold to the Central Railroad of New Jersey. — Walter A. Lucas Collection

ney to San Francisco on the ship *Mary Robinson*. After a rough voyage around the Horn, the locomotives were landed in San Francisco in mid-1863 and there transferred to river steamers which brought them to Sacramento.

The two locomotives were soon at work hauling construction trains on the Central Pacific, which was advancing east towards the foothills of the Sierra Nevada mountains. C. P. No. 3, the *C. P. Huntington* was a 4-2-4 tank-frame engine, with a four-wheel trailer truck carrying the weight of the fuel and water, whereas No. 4, the *T. D. Judah* was a 4-2-2 tender locomotive, with a two-wheel trailer truck and a six-wheel tender holding considerably more wood and water than that of the *C. P. Huntington*. By the time the Central Pacific reached the section of heavy grades east of Newcastle, the two "singles" were found to be sadly lacking in tractive effort, being of no use in hauling construction trains except on relatively level track. Photographs of the *C. P. Huntington* taken during the construction days invariably show it hauling one or two flat cars with seats for visitors, or a single passenger coach. After the Central Pacific was completed in 1869 and the railroad being equipped with over 175 locomotives, the *C. P. Huntington* was sold to a new railroad, the Southern Pacific of California where it became No. 1, the road's first locomotive. Its sister engine was sent to Oakland and for years hauled suburban trains between Berkeley and the Oakland Pier. By 1889 it had outlived its usefulness and was sold to the Wellington Colliery Company on Vancouver Island, British Columbia.

The Central Pacific inherited a third "single" when ten locomotives from the Western Pacific Railroad were added to its roster in 1870. All of the W. P.'s locomotives were 4-4-0s except engine J, the *Wm. Penn*, which was a 4-2-0 T type built in 1835 by William Norris for the Philadelphia & Columbia Railroad, later running on the Strasburg Railroad in Lancaster County, Pennsylvania. The Strasburg sold it to the Norris-Lancaster Locomotive Works who rebuilt and re-sold the engine to the Western Pacific in 1865. As Central Pacific No. 175, it was smaller than the *C. P. Huntington*. With a pair of 54-inch drivers and 10x18-inch cylinders, it was of little use except as a switcher. In 1885 it was sold to the Pacific Iron & Nail Co. of Oakland, California, where it worked for ten years, then retired to a junkyard where it remained for years before being scrapped.

Digressing from the story of the *C. P. Huntington* for a moment, mention of two California built "singles" should be made here. In May 1867, the Vulcan Iron Works of San Francisco turned out a 2-2-0 locomotive with four-wheel tender for the

The first known photo of the "C. P. Huntington," hauling a train of sightseers during the early construction days of the Central Pacific. The engine had no headlight at the time as it never ran at night. — G. M. BEST COLLECTION

Central Pacific No. 4, the "T. D. Judah" had a two-wheel trailer truck under the cab, and an oddly designed tender. — G. M. BEST COLLECTION (*Below*) Western Pacific's "Wm. Penn" was already 25 years old when photographed at the Norris-Lancaster Works in Pennsylvania. Rebuilt from parts of a William Norris engine built in 1835, the "Wm. Penn" was shipped to California in 1865. — THOMAS NORRELL COLLECTION

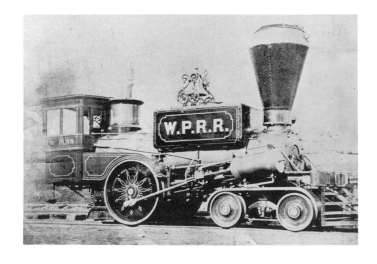

Napa Valley Railroad. Named the *Calistoga*, it served a short time on that line, then was sold to the Vaca Valley & Clear Lake Railroad, where it was renamed *Vacaville* No. 1. With 62-inch drivers and 9x18-inch cylinders, it had less tractive effort than the Danforth & Cooke engines although it could haul two-car passenger trains over the level track of the railroad along the west side of the Sacramento River basin. This engine served its second owners until 1888, when it was sold to the Union Coal Company and disappeared from historical records. Another "single" by the same builder was delivered in 1869 to the Los Angeles & San Pedro Railroad, being the first locomotive in Southern California. Named the *San Gabriel*, its life was short. The story goes that the boiler exploded at the time the engine was first fired up; this may be true but nevertheless it was in service during the early months of the railroad's operation. It was laid aside as soon as three Schenectady built 4-4-0's arrived early in 1870, and its fate is unknown.

Older than the Vulcan Iron Works engines were four steam cars built by the Fulton Iron Works of San Francisco in 1860 for the Market Street Railroad. The power unit in the front end was a 2-2-0 locomotive with a pair of solid 36-inch driving wheels and three of the four cars had horizontal boilers, the first one having a vertical boiler. The rear of the coach was supported by the usual 4-wheel passenger car truck. After these cars were replaced by cable cars, some of the power units were equipped with cabs and converted to industrial locomotives.

The other pair of Danforth & Cooke "singles" built at the same time as the two sold to the Central Pacific were purchased by the Oregon Steam Navigation Company, a 5-foot gauge road then building between The Dalles and the town of

Vaca Valley & Clear Lake No. 1, the "Vacaville" built by the Vulcan Iron Works of San Francisco in 1867. *(Below)* The Los Angeles & San Pedro Railroad locomotive "San Gabriel," the first engine in Southern California. This was built by the Vulcan Iron Works in 1869. — BOTH G. M. BEST COLLECTION

— SAN GABRIEL —
THE PIONEER LOCOMOTIVE OF LOS ANGELES COUNTY
CYLINDERS 9 x 18 INCHES ——— DRIVERS 5 FEET 2 INCHES

Oregon Steam Navigation Company No. 2, the "D. F. Bradford" at The Dalles, Oregon, in 1866. Note the interesting painting on the side of the tender. — DON H. ROBERTS COLLECTION.

Celilo in Oregon Territory, a distance of 15 miles along the gorge of the Columbia River. Named the *J. C. Ainsworth* and the *D. F. Bradford*, both engines were 4-2-2 tank frame engines with 54-inch drivers and 11x15-inch cylinders, identical in every respect with the *C. P. Huntington*. When the railroad was acquired by the Oregon Railway & Navigation Company in 1879, the two engines became O.R.&N. Nos. 1 and 2. The new owners held them in such low regard that both locomotives were retired in October 1885. Company records state that both were scrapped at that time. However, a photograph in an album showing construction scenes on the Pachuca & Tampico Railroad in Mexico around the turn of the century shows a "single" almost a carbon copy of either of the two Oregon Steam Navigation Company engines. All of which leads to the conclusion that at least one of these engines was sold as an operating locomotive to the contractor building the Pachuca & Tampico.

The *C. P. Huntington* fared better than its sisters, perhaps because it found its way to San Jose and served for many years on a local train from there to Hollister, California, a level run with two or three coaches. After 15 years of active service around San Jose, it was transferred to Oakland commute service for a while, then was sent to Sacramento as "too light for passenger service". It was renumbered No. 1001 in 1891 when all the locomotives of the railroads controlled by the Southern Pacific were renumbered into one common system, although photos of the engine taken during the 1890's show that it was never renumbered, probably because it was assumed the engine would never run on the main line again. At Sacramento it was used in work train service where speed was no requirement. In 1897 it was converted into a weed burner with an oil tank mounted on

Oregon Steam Navigation Company "J. C. Ainsworth," a sister engine of the "C. P. Huntington". — D. L. STEARNS COLLECTION

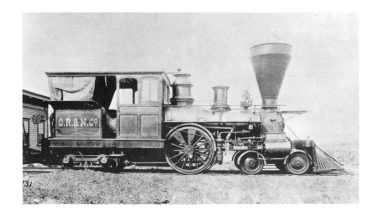

Oregon Railway & Navigation Company No. 1, formerly the "J. C. Ainsworth" in its last days before sale or scrapping. — DON H. ROBERTS COLLECTION

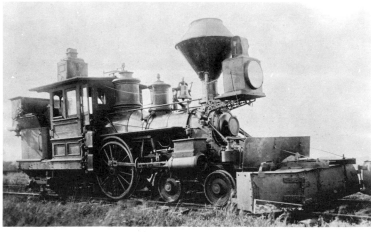

In the view above, the "C. P. Huntington" as seen during its halcyon days at San Jose, ready for a run to Hollister with the daily local. *(Upper Right)* The "C. P. Huntington" as a weed burner in 1898. The engine was being stored at the Sacramento shops. — Both G. M. Best Collection

The "C. P. Huntington" in work train service during 1890. The engine is pushing a pile driver into position for bridge repairs after a washout near Lodi. *(Below)* Southern Pacific No. 1 after its first restoration in the Sacramento shop grounds. — Both G. M. Best Collection

top of the tender and a huge flame thrower supported by the pilot beam. In this lowly service it worked until June 1900, at which time it was condemned and ordered scrapped. Officially, the engine was scrapped, but as in the case of a small shop goat many years later, the boys around the Sacramento shops were sentimental about the engine. The locomotive was shoved way back into the tender shop toward the end of a stall, completely concealed from view by any visiting brass hats. There it sat for five years, during which it was robbed of its bell, the pilot, and other parts which were needed for other engines.

In 1906 approval was given by the Master Mechanic to an employee suggested plan to move the engine out of hiding, then restore its missing external parts, after which it was painted by voluntary labor and placed in the shop grounds for all the employees to see. There it stood until 1914 when it had attracted sufficient attention from an economy minded management to be condemned once more. It was ordered moved to the scrap dock and cut up without further ceremony. Like the proverbial telephone call to the Warden of the prison just as the condemned man is about to be hanged, the San Francisco headquarters office suddenly decided to restore the engine and exhibit it at the Panama Pacific Exposition to be held in San Francisco the following year. The hasty telephone call to Sacramento was made just in time. The *C. P. Huntington* was again brought into the backshop and completely restored. Early in 1915, the engine was loaded on a flat car and shipped to the Exposition. The train was handled by one of the newest cab-ahead mallet compounds.

Central Pacific No. 4 the "T. D. Judah" at Berkeley. It was its last days as a double-ender hauling commute trains. — G. M. BEST COLLECTION (Below) In operating condition for the first time since 1900, the "C. P. Huntington" poses at the Sacramento roundhouse during 1922. — D. L. JOSYLN

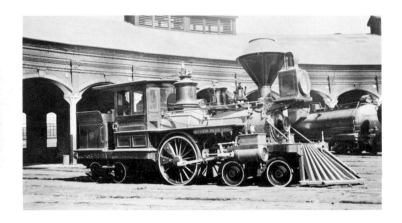

At the Fair, the *C. P. Huntington* was exhibited as the first locomotive on the Southern Pacific, which it certainly was, although the locomotive *Governor Stanford* was the first Central Pacific locomotive. This engine had for many years been preserved in a museum at Stanford University. The *C. P. Huntington* thus became a symbol in the eyes of Southern Pacific management and when it was returned to Sacramento in 1916, it was placed on the lawn in front of the station. There it remained until 1922 when an old locomotive was needed for a "Days of 49" celebration in Sacramento. Such a locomotive would have to be in operating condition, so the *C. P. Huntington* was taken to the back shops, given a complete boiler overhaul and was placed in service during the festivities. The *C. P. Huntington* pulled an open flat car through the streets of the city, with appropriately costumed passengers simulating the trains of visitors the engine hauled during construction days in the 1860's. Since the engine was now in good operating condition, it was used from time to time for other celebrations. In 1925 it appeared in a motion picture called the *Iron Horse*. At the picture's premiere at the Egyptian Theater in Hollywood, the *C. P. Huntington* was exhibited in the outdoor foyer of the theater throughout the run of the picture. Between jobs, the engine was stored under canvas on a special platform in one of the Sacramento shop buildings, for it was now a valuable property; no longer the waif which hid in dark corners and eluded the men with the acetylene torch.

Comparison view of the "C. P. Huntington" and Southern Pacific No. 4340 on occasion of the C.P.'s first day in steam, April 10, 1926. — D. L. JOSLYN

Among its many journeys was a trip to Oregon when the S. P. Cascade line was opened in 1927; an appearance in New Orleans during the opening of the new Huey Long Bridge across the Mississippi, and a parade down the streets of Sacramento when Governor James Rolph was inaugurated. Whenever new locomotives were built at the Sacramento shops or were received from the Baldwin Locomotive Works, the *C. P. Huntington* was hauled out and set alongside the new steamers to

show the comparison between 1863 and modern times. Between 1933 and 1934 it appeared under steam in the transportation pageant staged by Edward Hungerford at the Century of Progress Exposition in Chicago, sharing the spotlight with another "single", the *Pioneer* of the Cumberland Valley Railroad.

Its last appearance under steam was at Los Angeles in May 1939, on the occasion of the opening of the Los Angeles Union Passenger Terminal. A pageant of sorts was staged for three nights before the station was opened for business. Prior to the pageant, a mammoth parade down Alameda Street used the main line of the Southern Pacific from the old Central Station to the junction of the northern and eastern lines of the railroad. The *C. P. Huntington* hauling one of the old Virginia & Truckee coaches owned by Paramount Studios, was in the vanguard. The writer was fortunate enough to be present when the engine was tried out at Taylor Roundhouse before the parade, and was privileged to not only throw cordwood into the firebox, but run the engine a half mile from the north ladder track to the roundhouse turntable lead. Although the I.C.C. had generously extended the date of flue expiration to permit the engine to run in the pageant, the boiler pressure maximum had been reduced to 110 lbs. On a relatively

The little "C. P. Huntington" is dwarfed by one of the new Cab-In-Front type articulated steam locomotives on March 23, 1937.   D. L. JOSLYN (*Below*) At Los Angeles in May 1939, the author poses with the "C. P. Huntington" at Taylor roundhouse before it was placed under steam. — G. M. BEST

Nearly 50 years of steam locomotive development on Southern Pacific is shown in the above illustration taken at the Sacramento Shops. — SOUTHERN PACIFIC COLLECTION

smooth track it rode like a springless rubble car, for the springs had become hard and brittle. Rough ride or not, Shop Foreman L. D. Hoyal was at the throttle during the parade and enjoyed every minute of the trip.

After the three-day pageant at the station was concluded, the *C. P. Huntington* was loaded on a flat car and returned to Sacramento. Since the boiler shell was — to use a charitable phrase — in a "delicate condition", it was decided to permanently retire the engine from active service; either that or a new boiler, a horrible compromise, as it would automatically remove half of the historic engine from the scene. Back on the Sacramento station platform, it was protected from the weather by a shed with open sides and until 1964 was on exhibit there. In 1956 it was joined by Southern Pacific No. 4294, the last steam locomotive to be built expressly for the railroad. Thus were the first and last Southern Pacific steam locomotives saved from oblivion. To make way for a freeway which will take part of the lawn of the station, the *C. P.*

Huntington has been moved to the State Fairgrounds and has been presented to the State of California as a permanent gift.

So ends the saga of the Danforth & Cooke "singles" of 1863 and the sole survivor, now 102 years old. The *C. P. Huntington* will remain as a reminder that in the city of Paterson, New Jersey in 1863, they built locomotives which were in the maker's advertising, "warranted if well used"!

❧◖❀◗❧

A great part of the information contained in this narrative was given to the writer by the late David L. Joslyn during the last 30 years of his life. His priceless story of the *C. P. Huntington* in Railway & Locomotive Historical Society Bulletin No. 61 published in 1943 represented his experience with the engine from 1902 until its retirement to the Sacramento depot lawn in 1940. Dave loved this engine, and the drawings of the engine which have been preserved by the Southern Pacific were the work of his pen.

Index

Allis-Corliss Generator, 98
American Car Company, 77
American Locomotive Company, 104
American Railroad Journal, 5-7
American Transportation, 87

Baker, Richard S., 79
Baldwin Locomotive Works, 23, 110
Baltimore, City of,
  Baltimore & Ohio Railroad, 86-109
  Belt Line Railroad, 86-109
  Canton, 89
  City College, 90
  Howard Street Tunnel, 87-109
  Locust Point, 89
  Maryland Art Institute, 109
  Mount Royal, 91
  Mount Royal Station, 92, 98, 100-102,
    109
  New Civic Center, 100
  Patapsco River, 89
  Pennsylvania Railroad, 89-90
  Union Station, 89
Baltimore Clipper, 87
Baltimore Sun, 92
Baltimore & Ohio Railroad, 24, 86-109
  Baltimore Belt Line Railroad, 88-89
  Bay View Junction, 91
  Bolton Lot, 99
  Camden Station, 89-92, 95-96, 98-100,
    104-109
  Electric Locomotives, 86-109
  Electrification, 86-109
  Fair of the Iron Horse, 107 108
  Gauntlet Track, 107, 109
  Howard Street Tunnel, 89-109
  Mount Clare Shops, 107
  Mount Royal Station, 92, 98, 100-102,
    109
  Mount Winans, 109
  Old Maude, 24
  Powerhouse, 98
  Railway Tunnel, 86-109
  RDC-Rail Diesel Car, 109
  Royal Blue, 95
  Royal Blue Line, 102
  Transportation Museum, 107
  Tunnel Signals, 107
  Waverly Tower, 98
Baltimore Sun, 92
Baltimore Transit Company, 107
Beebe, Lucius, 10
Beeler, J. O., 73, 75, 84
Best, Gerald M., 110
  Big Boy, 21
Birney, Charles, 77
Birney Safety Car, 67, 76-85
Book of Rules, 12
Boston Locomotive Works, 110, 117
Boston Transcript, 90
Broadway Limited, 10
Bus (Motor Vehicle)
  Stanley Steamer, 75
  White Motor Rail Bus, 75
Bussard Bus Company, 84

Cab-In-Front Locomotive, 23-24, 117-118
California, State of, 27
  Alturas, 31-32
  Berkeley, 112, 116
  Donner Pass, 33
  Hollister, 114-115

  Hollywood, 116
  Los Angeles, 33, 116-117
  Newcastle, 112
  Oakland, 112, 114
  Ravondale, 32
  Sacramento, 33, 114, 116-118
  San Francisco, 112, 114
  San Joaquin Valley, 33
  San Jose, 114-115
  State Fair Grounds, 118
  Turlock, 31
Canada, 15
  Vancouver Island, B.C., 112
Canadian National Railway, 14-15
Casey Jones, 13, 21
Catechism of the Locomotive, 7
Central Pacific Railroad, 110-112
Central Railroad of New Jersey, 111
Century of Progress Exposition, 117
Civil War, 110
Cleveland, Painesville & Ashtabula R.R.,
  110
Colorado, State of,
  A&M College, 69
  Boulder, 68
  Cripple Creek, 68
  Curecanti Needle, 35
  Denver, 68
  Fort Collins, 67-85
  Greeley, 76
  Gunnison River, 35
  Larimer County, 71
  Longmont, 68
  Loveland, 68
  Pioneer Museum, 79, 85
  Pueblo, 68
  Victor, 68
Colorado & Southern Railway, 68-75,
  80, 84
Colorado Springs & Cripple Creek
  District Ry., 68
Cumberland Valley Railroad, 110, 117

Danforth & Cooke Locomotive Works,
  110-111, 113, 118
Daylight, Coast Limited, 23, 27
Daylight, San Joaquin Limited, 31
Denver & Interurban Railroad, 68-85
Denver & Rio Grande Railroad, 18, 34
Denver Tramway, 70, 81
Detroit River Tunnel Company, 104
Dieselization, 33
Duke, Donald, 10, 87

Eddy, Harry L., 7
Edmunds, W. H., 75
Electrification, Railways,
  Box Cabs — Locomotive, 104
  Cable Traction, 91
  Contact Shoe Collector, 97-98
  General Electric Co., 89
  GG-1 Locomotive, 92
  Locomotives, 87-109
  Motors, 93-94
  Overhead Collection, 91
  Overhead Supports, 97
  Pantograph, 94, 97
  Power Distribution, 96
  Powerhouse, 98
  Railroads, 87-109
  Steeple Cab — Locomotives, 93-94
  Street Railways, 67-85
  Third Rail System, 98

  Trough Overhead Collection, 94
Elevated Railroads, 89
Erie Railroad, 12

Forney, M. N., 7
Fort Collins, Colorado, 67-85
Fort Collins *Express,* 68-69, 70, 76
Fort Collins *Express Courier,* 80
Fort Collins Municipal Railway, 67-85
Franklin Institute, 7
Fulton Iron Works, 113

General Electric Company, 89, 91,
  93-94, 96-98, 104, 106-107
Grand Central Terminal, 100
Great Western Ry. of England, 110
Greeley Electric Railway, 81
Guaranty Trust Co. of New York, 75

Harper's Weekly, 13
Heller, Martin V., 110
Hoyal, L. D., 118
Hubbard, Freeman, 13, 35, 37
Hungerford, Edward, 100, 117
Huntington, Collis P., 110

Iron Horse — Motion Picture, 116

Jewett Street Car Co., 71
Jones, Billy, 21
Joslyn, David L., 118

King of the Rails, 21

Lake Shore & Michigan Southern R.R.,
  111
Last of the Birneys, 66-85
Leslie, Frank, *Illustrated Newspaper,*
  13, 35
Library of Congress, 7
Lima Locomotive Works, 23-26
  A-1 Locomotive, 25
  Super Power Locomotive, 24-25, 33
Locomotive, The Locomotive Engineer,
  10-21
Locomotives, Diesel, 21
Locomotives, Electric, 87-109
Locomotives, Steam,
  A-1, 25
  American Type (4-4-0), 19, 110
  Automatic Stoker, 19, 30
  Articulated Type, 21-33
  Backhead, 19
  Booster, 25
  Cab, 12, 16, 30
  Cab-In-Front Type, 23-24, 27, 117-118
  Climax, 36
  Coal Burning, 23-33
  Consolidation Type (2-8-0), 33
  Crossheads, 30
  Cylinders, 28
  Driving Rods, 30
  Engineers, 10-21
  Feedwater Heater, 28
  Firebox, 28

Fireman, 18
General Steel Casting, 33
Heisler, 36
Hostler, 18-19
Injector, 28
K-4 Type, 10
Lubricator, 28
Mallet Type, 24-25
Northern Type (4-8-4), 23, 27
Oil Burning, 21, 25
Pacific Type, (4-6-2), 10
Passenger, 23
Roundhouse, 18-19
Shay, 36
Single Drivered, 110-118
Superheater, 25
Tender, 30, 33
Utilization, 13
Walschaert Valve Gear, 28
Whistle, 13
Wipers, 18
Locomotives, Steam (By Name),
    J. C. Ainsworth, 114
    Big Boy, 21
    D. F. Bradford, 114
    Calistoga, 113
    S. M. Craver, 111
    DeWitt Clinton, 12
    C. P. Huntington, 110-118
    T. D. Judah, 110, 112, 116
    Old Maude, 24
    Wm. Penn, 112
    Pioneer, 18, 110, 117
    San Gabriel, 113
    Governor Stanford, 116
    Tiger, 18
    Vacaville, 113
Los Angeles & San Pedro Railroad, 113
Los Angeles Union Passenger Terminal,
    117

Market Street Railroad, 113
Maryland,
    Baltimore, 86-109
Maryland Central Railroad, 90
Maryland Construction Company, 90
Michigan Central Railroad, 104
Milwaukee Road, 36
Minor, D. K., 7
Mister Espee, 24
Monthly Journal, 12
Moorman, R. A., 66

Napa Valley Railroad, 113
National Car Company, 79
Nevada, State of, 27
    Fernley, 32-33
    Pyramid Lake, 32
    Smoke Creek Desert, 32
    Sparks, 33
Nevada Northern Railway, 4
New Mexico, State of, 30
    Corona, 25
    Dawson Field, 25, 33
    French, 33
    Gallina, 25
    Tucumcari, 25, 33
New York American, 6
New York & Erie Railroad, 110
New York Central & Hudson River R.R.,
    16
New York Central — Grand Central
    Terminal, 100

New York, State of,
    Greycourt, 110
    Port Jervis, 110
Night Train, 15
Norris-Lancaster Locomotive Works, 112
Norris, William, Locomotive Works, 112

Oregon Railway & Navigation Co., 114
Oregon, State of, 33
    Celilo, 114
    Columbia River, 114
    The Dalles, 113
    Klamath Falls, 33
Oregon Steam Navigation Co., 113-114

Pachuca & Tampico Railroad, 114
Pacific Iron and Nail Co., 112
Panama Pacific Exposition, 115
Pennsylvania Railroad, 10, 24, 89, 90, 92
Peyton, Ernest S., 66
Philadelphia & Columbia R.R., 112
Philadelphia Press, 90
Pioneer Museum, 79
Poem — *The Electric Locomotive,* 109
Poor, H. V., 7
Prairie King, 18
Pullman, 37

Quiz on Railroads & Railroading, 21

Railroad,
    Boomer, 36-37
    Dieselization, 33
    Electrification, 86-109
    Language, 35-65
    Modernization, 23, 35
Railroad Advocate, 7
Railroad Avenue, 13, 37
Railroad Gazette, 94, 96
Railroad Magazine, 36-37
Railroad Stories, 36
Railroad & Engineering Journal, 7
Railroaders' Lingo, 35-65
Railway & Locomotive Historical
    Society, 118
Railways, Street, 67-85
Rensselaer & Saratoga R.R., 111
Rock Island Line, 29
Rolph, James, 117
Royal Blue, 95

Sailing Ships,
    Mary Robinson, 111
    Success, 110
Santa Fe Railway, 33
Saturday Evening Post, 82
Single Drivered Steam Locomotives in
    the West, 110-118
Smithsonian Institution, 110
Southern Pacific, 8, 22-33, 110-118
    AC-9 Type, 27
    Bulletin, 21
    Cab-In-Front Type, 23-24, 27, 32,
        117-118
    Cascade Line, 117
    Daylight, 23, 27
    Golden State Route, 29

C. P. Huntington, 110-112, 114-118
T. D. Judah, 110, 112, 116
Likely "S" Grade, 32
Locomotives of, 22-33, 110-118
Modoc Line, 32-33
Rio Grande Division, 25, 27, 31, 33
Sacramento Shops, 28, 116-118
San Joaquin Daylight, 31
Governor Stanford, 116
3400 Class (2-8-0), 33
3800 Class (2-8-4), 22-33
4400 Class (4-8-4), 23
Southern Pacific of California, 112
Stanford University, 116
Stanley Steamer, 75
Steam Locomotive Engineering, 87, 96
Strasburg Railroad, 112
Street Car Manufacturers,
    American Car Company, 77
    Jewett Manufacturing Co., 71
    National Car Company, 79
    Stone & Webster Syndicate, 77
    Woeber Carriage Works, 69-70
Street Car Types,
    Birney Type, 67-85
    One-Man Type, 73
    P.C.C. Type, 85
Street Railways, 67-85

Tales of An Engineer, 18
Texas, State of, 25
    El Paso, 25, 33
Transportation Heritage, 5
Traveltown (Los Angeles), 115
Trolley Car, 66-85
Tunnels,
    Baltimore Belt Line, 87-109
    Howard Street, 87-109
    Maryland Construction Co., 90
Two-Eight-Eight-Four, 23-33

Union Coal Company, 113
Union Pacific Railroad, 21
United States Military Railroad, 110
United States Railroad Administration,
    74

Vaca Valley & Clear Lake R.R., 113
Valentine, Roger, 23
Virginia & Truckee Railroad, 75, 117
Virginia Transit Authority, 84
Vulcan Iron Works, 112-113

Warman, Cy, 18
Wellington Colliery Co., 112
Western Light & Power Company, 77
Western Pacific Railroad, 112
Westinghouse Air Brakes, 30
White Motor Company, 75
Wilmarth, Seth, 110
Woeber Carriage Works, 69-71
Wonders & Curiosities of the Railway,
    12
World War I, 36
Wyoming, State of,
    Cheyenne, 68, 80
    Sherman Hill, 21

LAYOUT - DON DUKE

HALFTONES - AL ROSE